Faith's Fundamentals

Seven Essentials
of Christian Belief

Faith's Fundamentals

Seven

Essentials

of

Christian

Belief

By Jack Cottrell

STANDARD
PUBLISHING
Cincinnati, Ohio

Cover design by Listenberger Design Associates

The Standard Publishing Company, Cincinnati, Ohio.
A division of Standex International Corporation.

02 01 00 99 98 97 96   5 4 3 2

Library of Congress Cataloging-in-Publication Data

Cottrell, Jack.
    Faith's fundamentals : seven essentials of Christian belief / Jack Cottrell.
        p.   cm.
    Includes bibliographical references.
    ISBN 0-7847-0390-6
    1. Theology, Doctrinal--Popular works. I. Title.
BT77.C785 1995
230--dc20   95-7837
                                             CIP

Contents

Introduction..9

1. Truth Itself Is Fundamental..11

2. God Is Real...23

3. The Bible Is God's Word...33

4. Jesus Is Our Savior...45

5. Jesus Is God's Son...57

6. We Are Saved by Grace, Through Faith, in Baptism............71

7. Jesus Is Coming Again...83

Introduction

Putting on the Armor

Spiritual warfare is a topic that has received a lot of attention lately. This is good. We must never forget that "our struggle is not against flesh and blood, but against the rulers, against the powers, against the world forces of this darkness, against the spiritual forces of wickedness in the heavenly places" (Ephesians 6:12). These "spiritual forces" are Satan and his demons.

Each Christian is a personal target of Satan, marked for conquest. The devil's goal is to strip us of our saving faith in Christ. He is working hard to overthrow the church itself, to dilute its influence and to render it ineffective in its mission.

Satan works through various means, but the main weapon he uses against us is falsehood or false teaching. The Bible characterizes Satan as a deceiver and a liar more than anything else. He "deceives the whole world" (Revelation 12:9). He deflects the truth from people's hearts "that they may not believe and be saved" (Luke 8:12). Evil spirits work through false prophets (1 John 4:1-3). Many will fall prey to "deceitful spirits and doctrines of demons" (1 Timothy 4:1). Jesus said the devil "does not stand in the truth, because there is no truth in him"; "he is a liar, and the father of lies" (John 8:44).

False doctrine is not just an inert, impersonal, passive possibility that we can avoid as long as we do not actively pursue it.

No! As an instrument of Satan, it is something he throws in our path to cause us to stumble. It is something he chases us with, to throw over our heads like a net or a lariat.

If we are not actively and consciously defending ourselves against "the schemes of the devil" (Ephesians 6:11), we will surely become his captives.

But we need not despair, for God has provided us with all the armor and weaponry we need for such a defense. Ephesians 6 speaks of "the full armor of God" that enables us to resist the devil (v. 13). Each piece of the armor is important, but it seems clear that *knowledge of the truth* is the primary means of defense against the great deceiver. The very first piece of armor to put on is truth: "having girded your loins with truth" (v. 14). Then we are told to take up the "sword of the Spirit, which is the word of God" (v. 17).

What does this mean? For a successful defense against deceitful spirits and doctrines of demons, it is not enough just to *have* the Word of God, in the sense of owning a Bible. It is not enough simply to know its contents, with Bible knowledge being only a mental exercise. It is not enough just to have a passive, implicit faith in its contents, or to say, "Sure, I believe whatever the Bible says."

Of course, we must know the teaching of God's Word, and we must believe it as truth. But we must also know that this truth is our only sure weapon against the deadly attacks of Satan, and we must love it (2 Thessalonians 2:10) and guard it and wield it boldly in our personal lives and in the church.

In this little book I am presupposing the existence and value of truth or sound doctrine. My goal is to identify and explain the essential core of Christian doctrine, the "point of the sword," so to speak. That other doctrines are not discussed here does not imply their unimportance or irrelevance. Indeed, all Scripture is God-breathed and is therefore the one true measure for sound doctrine and holy living (see 2 Timothy 3:16, 17). But without the seven doctrines discussed here, all the rest is futile. To espouse a "Christianity" that does not include these truths is like putting on "armor" made of cardboard and carrying a rubber "sword."

May studying this book make you better equipped to stand firm against the deceiver. May you think of it as tightening your armor about you, and sharpening your sword.

Fundamental #1

Truth Itself Is Fundamental

The "fundamentals" are the essential truths of the Christian faith, the foundational principles on which our faith stands. The seven basic doctrines that fall into this category are the subject of this book. The first of these is that *truth itself is fundamental.*

Four Questions About Truth

Not everyone has studied philosophy, but we all have to do some informal philosophizing once in a while. That is true just now, as we ask four crucial questions about this abstract thing called "truth."

Does Truth Exist?

Pilate is famous for asking, "What is truth?" (John 18:38). Some may think this is the most basic of all questions, but even more fundamental is the question, Does truth even exist?

Probably the most pervasive characteristic of our modern culture is its abandonment of absolutes. "Truth" is relative to particular times, places, and people. What is true for you in your cultural context may be false for me in my situation. What is true for you today may be false for you tomorrow.

This view goes by various names: relativism, contextualism, situationalism, multiculturalism. The main point is the denial of absolute truth in any significant sense.

If this view is *true* (note the inherent contradiction!), then it has the most drastic consequences. For example, history can be rewritten at will. Schools can abandon fact-oriented curricula and focus on behavior modification. Teachers' views are no more "correct" than students'; parents' decisions are no more "right" than those of their children. No one's conduct can be criticized; neither Hitler nor idol-worshippers can be condemned. When you are ill, it won't really matter what medicine you take.

In the end all that matters is what you *like* or *value*. If someone else likes or values something different, that's fine. If there is a conflict, the subjective values of the strongest group or individual will prevail. Might will make right.

The fact is, however, that relativism is a false view. It even contradicts itself by saying, "There is no absolute truth," since it is setting this statement forth as absolute truth.

Francis Schaeffer has pointed out that those who reject absolutes, thus denying the distinction between truth and falsehood, cannot live consistently with this belief. He cites the famous example of the composer John Cage, whose commitment to pure chance was so strong that he believed that no one musical note or sequence or combination of notes is better than any other. Thus he chose his notes by pure chance. However, as a mushroom connoisseur, he knew he might die if he picked and ate mushrooms at random, regardless of their shape, size, or color. Hence when he gathered mushrooms, he went strictly by the book, in contradiction to his asserted relativism.[1]

As Elton Trueblood points out, the existence of objective truth is clearly established by the abundant existence of *error*. Newspapers print corrections and retractions; students give wrong answers on exams; we all have had errors of memory. Even the most ardent denier of truth would complain if you picked up his briefcase or her purse by mistake. But as Trueblood explains, "We cannot be wrong unless there is something to be wrong *about!*" Unless there is truth, there can be no such thing as errors.[2]

The Bible often contrasts truth with error. The ninth commandment forbids false witness (Exodus 20:16). God's Word is truth (John 17:17). Those who deny the coming resurrection "have gone astray from the truth" (2 Timothy 2:18). In Acts 8, when Philip approached the chariot of the Ethiopian, the latter was reading from Isaiah. Philip's question presupposed the existence of truth: "Do you understand what you are reading?" (v. 30). If there is no such thing as truth, then one understanding is as good as another. If there is no truth, then the Athenians' "unknown God" (Acts 17:23) could just as well have been Baal as Yahweh.

Holding to the reality of truth is difficult in the face of militant relativism, but for Christians it is absolutely fundamental. Unbelievers generally gravitate toward relativism, especially with regard to ultimate questions, since it enables them to justify their wicked behavior (Romans 1:21-32). The only viewpoint they will *not* tolerate is the belief in absolute and exclusive truth. Hence early Christians were persecuted not so much for believing in Jesus, but for believing that all other gods and religions are false. Likewise, modern Bible believers ("right-wing fundamentalists") are singled out for attack not for their faith as such, but because their commitment to absolute truth makes them intolerant of false world views and false lifestyles.

What Is Truth?

Now we turn to Pilate's question, "What is truth?" This is not a request for a list of true statements, but a query concerning the *nature* of truth. What do we mean when we use this word? What determines whether a statement is true or not?

A common false answer to this question is associated with the philosophy called pragmatism. It says that a statement is true if it *works*, that is, if it accomplishes its purpose, if it brings about the desired effects. For example, to psych his soldiers up for a battle, a lieutenant may tell them of an act of astounding bravery by one of their fallen comrades. Though the officer knows it never really happened, it is considered to be truth because it inspires the soldiers to victory.

The only valid answer to Pilate's question, however, is known as the *correspondence* concept of truth. That is, a statement is true only if it corresponds to reality. A proposition can be called true if it describes what actually exists in reality. This approach to truth is one assumed by most people even if they have not thought about it formally.

Richard Bowman, a conservative Disciples of Christ minister and cofounder of Disciple Renewal, shows why it is crucial that we be aware of this distinction. He tells how his liberal seminary professors denied the actual reality of such things as the virgin birth, revelation, and heaven; but they taught that ministers should continue to affirm that such doctrines are *true*—not in the sense that they correspond to reality, but in the sense that they serve such purposes as giving people hope and keeping them committed to the church. (Of course, ministers need not disclose the fact that they are using a definition of *truth* totally different from that of most church members, who would probably be a bit upset if they knew it!) Thus ministers may confidently affirm that the doctrines of the virgin birth and the resurrection, for example, are *true*, while denying in their hearts that they actually happened![3]

This is in complete contrast with the Bible, which throughout assumes the correspondence concept of truth. For example, the resurrection of Jesus Christ is affirmed as an objective historical event, with the risen Savior appearing to hundreds of people in his recognizable bodily nature (1 Corinthians 15:5-7).

Paul declares that preaching the resurrection, if it did not really happen, is empty and vain and makes one a false witness. He says that believing the resurrection really happened, if it did not, is a vain and worthless faith that leaves one still in his sins (1 Corinthians 15:14-17). Claims to truth *work* (pragmatically) only when they correspond to *reality*.

What Is True?

For those who accept the answers given above to the first two questions, the next step is to sift through all competing claims to truth to determine which ones actually correspond to reality. In other words, which truth-claims are actually true?

Accepting a statement or claim as true is a decision that is always grounded in sufficient reason or sufficient evidence. In general, this is done in two ways.

First, we accept some things as true because we have personally experienced them. We *know* fire is hot, because we have been burned by it. We *know* what we had for breakfast today, since we (most of us, at least) were conscious when we ate it. Actually, only a small portion of what we regard as truth comes to us in this way.

Second, most of what we accept as true has come to us through the testimony of others. Technically speaking, all truth received in this way is a matter of *faith*. The data comes to us not through personal experience but through the reports of others, and we *believe* them.

Accepting someone else's testimony as true should not be a matter of "blind faith." We believe what others tell us only when we have good reason or evidence for doing so. Sometimes this is because we have reason to regard the sources as reliable and we simply take them at their word. This is why we generally believe what we read in a newspaper or news magazine. In other cases we may hear testimony but not accept it until we have found satisfactory corroborative evidence, which is what the state attempts to do in court cases.

The truths of the Christian faith come to us in this second way. They are reported by eyewitnesses such as the apostles (1 John 1:1-3), and by God himself speaking through the inspired authors of the Bible and in the person of Jesus Christ. We accept their testimony as true based on the abundant *evidence* available to us, as analyzed and set forth by Christian apologetics. This is in accord with the mandate of 1 Peter 3:15, that we should be able to "make a defense *[apologia]*" of our faith in Jesus Christ.

So in answer to the question, What is true? I maintain that the Christian world view as set forth in the Bible contains the basic truths concerning God and man and constitutes the basic framework for all other truth.

What Is Important Truth?

Many things—a seemingly infinite number of things—are true. But not all truths are important. I had a bagel for breakfast, but who cares? A duck-billed platypus is an egg-laying mammal, but who cares? Thus the last question we must ask about truth is this: What is *important* truth?

This applies not only to truth in general, but even to the vast amount of data found in the Bible itself. That Baal had 450 prophets calling on him at Mt. Carmel is true (1 Kings 18:19-22), but it is hardly crucial for Christian living. That Paul went through Sidon on his way to Rome is true (Acts 27:3), but surely it is not a matter of life and death.

So even with regard to biblical teaching, it is appropriate to ask, What is *important* truth? This book is an attempt to address this question, focusing especially on seven fundamental truths— including the truth that truth itself is fundamental.

Truths That Matter

We are simply being realistic when we recognize that some truths in Scripture are relatively less important than others. While accepting the whole Bible as true, Christians generally regard a certain core of biblical truth to be crucial and indispensable. Acknowledging this is not difficult; the hard part is trying to discern what these core truths are. In this section we will examine two attempts to do this.

"The Fundamentals"

In the late nineteenth and early twentieth centuries, theological liberalism spread like a cancer over Western Christendom. Doctrines that had been at the heart of Christian faith from its beginning were denied and tossed aside.

In reaction to this, orthodox Bible believers launched a spirited defense of traditional beliefs. Their overall strategy was clear. So as not to be distracted by arguments over less significant matters, they attempted to focus on what they considered to be the basics, the core doctrines of the Bible. Between 1910 and 1915 twelve booklets responding to liberal attacks and defending biblical truth were published under the general title of *The Fundamentals*.

Even before that time, various Christian groups were making attempts to identify the indispensable doctrines of the faith. Several versions were suggested, but the most common and representative list seems to be the following:

1. the verbal inspiration and inerrancy of the Bible
2. the virgin birth of Jesus Christ
3. his substitutionary atonement
4. his bodily resurrection
5. his visible second coming

Other items that were sometimes included were the deity of Christ and his miracle-working power.[4]

"In Essentials, Unity . . ."

A much quoted and revered formula suggesting that some doctrines are more important than others is this: "In essentials, unity; in nonessentials, liberty; in all things, love." Philip Schaff notes that this sentence has been traced to a 1627 tract by Rupertus

Meldenius, an orthodox Lutheran.[5] It was adopted by the founders of the Restoration Movement.

This slogan is still widely quoted and accepted in Christian churches and churches of Christ. The assumption is that biblical doctrines can be divided into two groups: essential doctrines, those necessary to be believed for salvation, and nonessential doctrines, which are not necessary for salvation.

Although the formula is generally accepted, there is no general agreement as to *which* doctrines should be considered essential. Many who discuss this issue define what they *mean* by "essentials," but do not venture a list of the specific doctrines that fall into this category. For example, one writer says that "essentials can only be those things that, if believed and practiced, result in our salvation," but he does not name them.

Among those who do suggest a list, there is no unanimity. One writer says the only essential is "Jesus is Lord," since this "includes everything that is necessary and excludes everything that is not necessary." A much more common suggestion is Peter's confession in Matthew 16:16, that Jesus is the Christ, the Son of the living God. As one writer said to me in a letter, "The *only* essential is that Jesus is the Christ, the son of the living God. *Everything* else is up for grabs." Others add the traditional plan of salvation. Still others include such things as the existence of God, his work of creation and providence, the deity of Christ, his atoning death and resurrection, godly living, and brotherly love.

How Do We Decide?

Determining which truths matter the most is no easy task. The personal or historical context within which the decision is made will certainly affect the outcome. For example, over against liberalism's rejection of a transcendent God and everything supernatural, the original fundamentalists tended to focus on the miraculous or supernatural elements of Christianity. The Restoration Movement's emphasis on the "essentials" slogan occurs in the context of denominationalism and reflects a fierce passion for unity. Fear of divisiveness no doubt accounts for the reluctance to compose a list, as well as the tendency to limit it to the lowest possible common denominator (Matthew 16:16, for instance).

But even Peter's confession was in response to a specific question occasioned by the circumstances of Jesus' ministry. The issue was not, "What is essential truth?" but, "Who exactly *is* Jesus of Nazareth, anyway?" Also, we must remember that Peter's answer was that of a devout Jew who as yet knew nothing of the saving work of Christ and the gospel plan of salvation.

In trying to decide what truths are absolutely basic, we must be careful not to allow ourselves to be overly influenced by a single narrow context. We must keep the whole scope of Scripture in mind and pay special attention to the Bible's own lists of basics (such as Ephesians 4:4-6 and Hebrews 6:1, 2) and to the content of the first sermons preached to unbelievers as recorded in the book of Acts.

Hitting the Bull's-Eye

On the surface, the concept of essential truth seems to be reasonable and necessary and straightforward. The fact is, however, that many things about it are vague and unclear. This is especially true of the slogan, "In essentials, unity; in nonessentials, liberty; in all things, love."

More seriously, this slogan is usually presented in a way that is misleading. In fact, as commonly explained, it has the effect of weakening and even destroying the very concept of truth or sound doctrine. It becomes a doorway to and and excuse for doctrinal relativism.

In this section we will take a look at some of the difficulties connected with the "essentials" slogan, and suggest an approach to this issue that preserves the reality and importance of truth.

A Problematic Slogan

To some it may seem almost blasphemous to call into question a slogan that has been so widely revered for so long. Nevertheless it must be done. In the first place, once the categories of essentials and nonessentials have been distinguished, it is not clear *how* we should decide which doctrines should go into which category.

I have seen dozens of articles and discussions about this question, and more than a half dozen different criteria suggested as the key to distinguishing between the categories. These include the following:

ESSENTIALS		NONESSENTIALS
Assertions of Scripture	(a)	*Interpretations* of Scripture
What is *specifically* asserted	(b)	*Application inferred* therefrom
Issues on which *God has spoken*	(c)	Issues on which *God is silent*
The *kerygma* (gospel as preached)	(d)	The *didache* (doctrine as taught)
The *simple or clear*	(e)	The *difficult or unclear*
Matters of *unanimous consent*	(f)	Matters *disagreed upon*
The *important*	(g)	The *unimportant*

These are all worthy suggestions, but there are many problems. Some of the suggestions involve subjective decisions (letters *d, e,* and *g*). Some simply beg the question (*f* and *g*). Most are much too inclusive; that is, if consistently applied, they would include far too many things in the "essentials" category *(a, b, c, e, f)*. Other difficulties could also be cited.

A second problem with the essentials-nonessentials principle is the status usually conferred upon doctrines placed in the latter category. Whether stated or not, "nonessential" by implication is usually equated with "unimportant."

This equation is reinforced by the common practice of altering the terminology of the slogan: "In matters of faith, unity; in matters of opinion, liberty; in all things, love." It is assumed that this means exactly the same things as the original slogan. This leads to the following conclusions: An essential is a matter of faith, that is, something that must be believed in order to be saved. A nonessential is the same as a matter of opinion. Therefore any belief that is not essential for salvation is a matter of opinion.

But what is a "matter of opinion"? This is usually taken to mean a conclusion that is more subjectively than objectively based, one that is based on preference or feeling rather than reason or evidence. In the context of Christian faith, an opinion is a matter upon which the Bible is silent, where there is neither a specific pronouncement nor a general principle that is relevant. "Matters of opinion" are issues for which opposite viewpoints are equally valid.

Thus when "opinion" is equated with "nonessential" in the slogan, this has a devastating effect on the whole concept of truth and sound doctrine. This is especially true since the "essentials" category is almost always a very short list ("Jesus is the Christ, the Son of God," for example). The practical result is that all other doctrines and assertions in the Bible are treated as unimportant matters for which there is no one correct understanding and where agreement or disagreement is irrelevant. In the words of the letter cited earlier, they are all "up for grabs."

This leads to the third general problem with the essentials-nonessentials, faith-opinion slogan—it creates the false impression that there are only two categories of doctrines: important ones that are essential for salvation and unimportant, nonessential matters of opinion. But this is seriously incorrect. Many teachings of Scripture that are not essential for salvation are nevertheless very important and in no way may be regarded simply as matters of opinion.

A Solution to the Problem

How is it possible to preserve the *reality* of truth and the concept of *essential* truth at the same time? One possible way would be simply to toss out the essentials-nonessentials slogan altogether. This is really not necessary, though, as long as we take care to understand and explain it properly. I suggest the following.

First, it would be best to completely abandon the "faith and opinion" terminology, since it causes more problems than it solves. Second, if we are going to keep the slogan as originally worded, we must give more serious thought to the meaning of the term *essentials.* It is not enough to limit it to "essential for salvation." A doctrine not essential *for salvation* is not by that fact alone a mere "nonessential." It may be essential or important for some other purpose.

In other words, we need to think in terms of different categories of "essential." We need to ask, "Essential *for what?*" Here are some valid possibilities: essential for salvation (to be sure), essential for Christian growth and maturity, essential for Christian joy and assurance, essential for a church leadership position, and essential to qualify as a congregation representing the true visible church.

At a recent convention, a speaker attempted to illustrate the essentials-nonessentials principle by referring to the way a target is laid out. Christian doctrine is like a target, he said, in that some things are the bull's-eye. These are the essentials. All other doctrines—the nonessentials or opinions—are like the concentric rings of the target. They may be in the tenth ring, or the thirty-fourth ring, or the ninety-eighth ring. Whatever the case, they are not the bull's-eye and are therefore not essential.

As presented, this illustration is faulty because, in reference to Christian doctrine, we have to consider not only the bull's-eye and the various concentric rings, but also the fact that some things are *off the board altogether.* As I see it, beliefs that are matters of opinion are not on the board at all—the Bible does not speak about them. Everything else is on the board, and everything on the board is *essential* for *something.* The bull's-eye doctrines are essential for salvation, but the concentric rings are essential for other things. (Leadership and maturity are two examples.)

Our basic concern is to preserve the concept of truth. True doctrines are true doctrines, whether they must be believed for salvation or not. Some may be peripheral or secondary, some may be important or necessary relative to a lesser purpose, and some may be crucial and critical for salvation itself. But all are *truth,* not *opinion.*

Hitting the Bull's-Eye

In this book we are dealing only with the bull's-eye truths, the doctrines at the very heart and core of Christian faith. The guiding criteria for choosing these truths are: (1) the items that were considered "fundamental" in the early twentieth-century polemic against liberalism, and (2) the items stressed in the evangelistic situations in the book of Acts, with special attention being given to the account of Philip and the Ethiopian eunuch in Acts 8:26-40.

To be sure, there is a lot more to the Christian faith than the items discussed here. The concentric rings on the board count too. But it is important for us to know what these bull's-eye doctrines are for three reasons.

First, discerning them as essential is important for the sake of our own salvation. These doctrines include what we personally must believe and practice for a right relationship with God.

Second, discerning these doctrines is important for settling the question of fellowship with other believers. If these things are essential for salvation, then whoever believes and practices them is also a Christian, our brother or sister in the Lord.

Third, knowing which doctrines are in the bull's-eye enables us to focus our efforts correctly in witnessing and evangelism. It helps us to not get sidetracked on issues that may be important for other things but not essential for salvation.

The doctrines we are focusing on in this study bring to mind the question, "If your house caught on fire, what would you save *first?*" Many expensive, beloved things would be passed over at first because some things simply take priority in this sort of situation—financial records, pictures, and mementos, for instance. In a similar way, we are dealing here with the "first things" of Christianity, the bull's-eye of Christian faith, its most fundamental truths.

[1] Francis Schaeffer, *The God Who Is There* (InterVarsity Press, 1968), 72–74.

[2] David Elton Trueblood, *General Philosophy* (1963; reprint, Grand Rapids: Baker Book House, 1976), 47–50.

[3] "Words and Their Meanings," *Disciple Renewal*, August 1987, 9–11.

[4] See Louis Gasper, *The Fundamentalist Movement 1930–1956* (1963; reprint, Grand Rapids: Baker Book House, 1981), 12, 13. Also see Millard Erickson, *The New Evangelical Theology* (Revell, 1968), 23.

[5] Philip Schaff, *History of the Christian Church,* VII: 650–653.

Fundamental #2

God Is Real

The German naturalist Alexander von Humboldt died in 1859 after a remarkable career of exploration and scientific investigation. His not-so-humble quest was to assemble "all knowledge of the physical world."[1] Needless to say, despite his vast achievements, he fell short of this goal.

We rightly smile at the futility of such an ambition. We know that the amount of potential knowledge in the physical world far exceeds the ability of any one man to accumulate and digest it. For that matter, given the difficulty of uncovering the past and the impossibility of knowing the future, it is safe to say that even the human race as a whole will never have "all knowledge of the physical world."

If this is true of the physical world, it is even more true for the nonphysical or spiritual world. The combined best efforts of human beings can never discover sure and certain truth about God, angels, the soul, morality, sin, and salvation.

In other words, it is one thing to say that truth is fundamental; it is another thing to say that this or that particular idea is true. This applies especially to the truths that we would consider to be the most crucial.

We may indeed be convinced that there is such a thing as

truth, contrary to the prevailing relativism. We may have the most sincere desire to possess that truth. But how? The humbling fact is this: It is possible *only* if God exists. God alone is the foundation of the very concept of truth, and he is the sole source of the most vital truths sought by man.

So in a real sense, the most basic fundamental is the fact that *God exists.*

God and Truth

The reason neither Humboldt nor any other human being could ever know all things, or even have all knowledge about even one thing, is that we are finite. Each individual is inherently limited by what is called the "egocentric predicament."

Our ego (our self, intellect, mind, or consciousness) is encased within a single small space, our skull, and it is encased within a single point of time, the now. This is the perspective from which we must view everything and from which all learning takes place. In general, all the ideas in our minds are filtered through our fallible senses and are maintained by our faulty memories. The future is not accessible to us at all, except by projection and guess. To top it all off, the certainty of death puts an unyielding limit on all our searches for truth.

Given this predicament, it is literally impossible for us to have absolute, 100 percent certainty about any matter of fact. In a sense, it is a wonder that we have any confidence at all in our knowledge and beliefs. Experience has shown us, though, that despite our limitations it is possible to have *practical* certainty about most things that have to do with everyday living.

For example, when you fill up your car with fuel, are you absolutely certain that you have received ten full gallons of gasoline just because the pump *says* ten gallons? Are you even certain that what you have put into your car is gasoline? Usually, in light of our past experience, the reputation of the station, and the government seal of approval, we accept these things as true even if our certainty is not technically absolute.

This inability to know truth absolutely may not be crucial when we are buying gasoline, but it becomes a more serious problem when the answer to a certain question may involve life and death. For example, is breathing gasoline fumes harmful? Do certain food additives cause cancer? What are the long-term side effects of certain medications? How much coffee is too much? Such questions are constantly being investigated, but even the best scientists cannot be absolutely sure about the answers.

The most serious jeopardy created by the egocentric predicament has to do with spiritual issues. For example, what is the true nature of man? Are we merely physical, or do we have souls or spirits? Do we have free will? Do we continue to exist after death? What is God like? Is there such a thing as "right and wrong"? If so, which actions are right and which are wrong? Are "wrong actions" sins against God? Will there be a judgment day? Do heaven and hell really exist? How can we be saved from sin?

There is a tremendous difference between these sorts of questions and the questions that can be investigated by the physical sciences. It is one thing to measure a gallon of gasoline or to analyze the consequences of breathing its fumes; it is a different thing to find the truth about sin, death, judgment, and salvation.

This is why the existence of God is fundamental. Man is finite, bound by an egocentric predicament, but God is not. God is infinite in every respect, including his knowledge. He is omniscient. He knows all things, and he knows them absolutely. His knowledge is complete and perfect. Absolute truth does exist: it is the contents of the mind of God.

This difference between God and man is rooted in the fact of creation. Man is in every respect a creature, and so is limited by nature. God alone is the Creator, the eternal one who brought man and everything else into existence out of nothing—*ex nihilo.* The distinction between Creator and creature is fundamental; it is the most important of all distinctions. The uncreated Creator is a unique kind of being. He transcends all the limitations by which creatures are inherently bound.

The existence of the transcendent Creator-God is the basis of absolutes of any kind. The mind of God is the prototype of all reason and logic. His very essence is *logos:* word, reason, logic (John 1:1). His infinite consciousness includes all possible knowledge about all things without gaps or errors. Thus everything he says about himself, the nature of man, right and wrong, sin and salvation, heaven and hell—is true. Thus God and God alone is the source of absolute truth.

Here is an important point. This connection between God and truth exists *only* if God is truly the *ex nihilo* Creator of everything distinct from himself. Only such a Creator-God truly transcends the limitations of finite beings such as we are. No other concept of God makes absolute truth possible. Without a Creator-God, we are doomed to relativism.

Only the Bible teaches a genuine concept of *ex nihilo* creation. "In the beginning God created the heavens and the earth" (Genesis 1:1). "All things came into being by Him" (John 1:3). He "calls into being that which does not exist" (Romans 4:17). Other religions may have myths of "creation," but not true creation from nothing. Only the God of Judeo-Christian belief is a true Creator and thus a valid basis for absolute truth.[2]

God and the Supernatural

One of Francis Schaeffer's most influential books is titled *The God Who Is There*. God truly exists—he is really there. But it is not enough to believe just that God *exists*. True belief in the true God includes the idea that he actually *intervenes* in our world and in our lives.

Not all concepts of God include this idea. For example, God is an important aspect of Aristotle's philosophy, but God's sole activity is thinking. And since he is God, the object of his thoughts can only be the highest and most sublime of all, namely, himself. Thus God's sole eternal activity is to think about himself. He is not even conscious of the world's existence.

According to Epicurus, another ancient philosopher, there are many gods—but they do not intervene in the world. They dwell in splendid isolation, "beautiful and happy and without thought of human affairs, eating and drinking and speaking Greek!"[3]

Some early American leaders espoused Deism. This view often included the idea that once God had created the world, he declined to have anything further to do with it.

Hebrews 11:6 tells us, however, that the faith that pleases God includes not only believing that "He is," but also "that He is a rewarder of those who seek Him." He is near to us. He is available to us. It is not futile to seek him. He himself enters our world to seek us, to find us, to reward us with gifts and fellowship and salvation. He has touched our world and our lives in miraculous and providential ways.

God's existence and his presence in the world are sometimes called the supernatural, in contrast with the natural world. The latter includes the world of physical nature and the events within it that occur as the result of natural laws. It also includes human beings and their thoughts and deeds.

Much confusion exists today about the existence of God and his relation to the so-called "supernatural." In this section we will try to clarify this relationship.

Natural "Gods"

A defining characteristic of the classical liberal theology in the early twentieth century was the denial of all the truly divine or supernatural aspects of Christianity. Liberals rejected miracles, revelation, and inspiration; they denied the incarnation, atonement, resurrection, and expected second coming of Jesus. They denied any real distinction between natural and supernatural—these are just two ways of looking at the same thing. In a sense everything is just a natural event, but in another sense everything is a miracle. In a sense Jesus was divine, but so is everyone else.

Why did liberals deny the presence of anything supernatural in the world? Basically, because they denied the existence of the transcendent Creator-God. They continued to speak of "God," but their god was patterned more after pantheism than the Bible. God is not separate from the world, but is wholly enclosed within it. In a sense the world *is* god. Everything is divine, or at least the divine is in everything. What men call "god" is just the most sublime aspect or dimension of nature.

This is what led the early fundamentalists to identify the inspiration of Scripture, the virgin birth of Christ, his atonement, his resurrection, and his second coming as the fundamentals. These are all crucial examples of the divine or supernatural elements of Christian faith. The existence of God is not specifically named as one of the fundamentals, but it is the basic presupposition of the ones that are named. By emphasizing these doctrines, the fundamentalists were repudiating any view that simply makes "god" a part of or identical with "nature."

The same situation still exists today. What many people think of as "God" is not even supernatural, but is just something that exists naturally as a part of the universe. When they say "God," they do not mean the living, personal, infinite Creator. Science-fiction writing sometimes includes encounters with "gods," but these turn out to be only incredibly advanced (evolved) beings from some other galaxy or dimension.

Sometimes this idea is presented as fact. In his book *Chariots of the Gods?* Erich von Daniken discusses belief in divine beings and the cause of many mysterious and allegedly supernatural events of the past, such as the "creation" of man. He says these things are all the result of regular visits to our planet by superintelligent alien beings in UFOs. This view is still popular.[4]

New Agers speak of "God," but the pantheistic god of the New Age movement is simply the entire universe (including human beings) when seen and understood in its truly natural state.

Let us be very clear about this. Contrary to views such as the above, the God of the Bible, the God who is real, is *not* in any sense a part of this natural world. Rather, as its Creator, he is distinct from it and infinitely transcends it in his essence and character. When for his purposes he enters this world and interacts with it, such events are truly supernatural. Only such a being as this is truly worthy to be called *God.*

"Supernatural" Creatures

Another point of confusion has to do with how we view the supernatural. Many people today believe in "the supernatural" without connecting it with God in any way. Of course, truly dedicated secularists (such as secular humanists) reject the existence of anything at all beyond the natural world. But many others believe in a spiritual world, a realm of spiritual beings whose powers are greater than ours and who sometimes interact with us. This is "the supernatural," but not "the divine." The beings who inhabit it are more like creatures than the Creator.

For some people, these spiritual beings are human beings who have died and whose spirits continue to exist in a higher and more energized plane. They continue to interact with us in various ways, either as mentors or tormentors. For others these spirits are inherently different from and superior to the human race. Sometimes they are called "angels," not in the biblical sense but in a spiritistic sense.

The concept of such "angels" who stand ready to assist us is popular today. In the darker realms of occultism, these spirits are closer to what we call "demons," whose powers are evoked for sinister purposes. This is the so-called world of the supernatural, and its often-miraculous manifestations in our natural world are thought of as supernatural events. Much religious belief and practice today is based not on God, but on this supernatural world.

Some still think of this as their religion, but a more popular term today is "spirituality." This term is more amenable to the absence of God and does not necessarily involve true worship.

What shall we say about this? First of all, it is quite true that such "supernatural" beings exist. They are not the spirits of deceased human beings, however. They are rather the invisible aspect of creation (Colossians 1:16), the angels. This includes the holy angels who serve God, as well as the fallen angels (2 Peter 2:4). The latter group includes Satan and the lesser fallen angels who serve him. These are called *evil spirits* and *demons*. They are the "principalities and powers" of which the Bible speaks. (See Ephesians 1:21; 2:2; 3:10; 6:12; Colossians 1:16; 2:15.)

Such beings are rightly called supernatural in the sense that they are not part of this natural, visible, physical world. Also, their powers are not limited by the laws of physics. So when they act within and upon this world, the results may indeed be supernatural or miraculous (2 Thessalonians 2:9).

Here is the second thing to remember, though. All such spiritual beings, whether angels or demons, are *creatures* just as we are. They have all the inherent limitations of created beings. They are finite or limited in their power and knowledge. No creature is or can be omniscient. Thus if such created "supernatural" beings are all that exist beyond ourselves, we are no better off than if only the natural world existed. For example, the existence of absolute truth would still be impossible.

The Divinely Supernatural

The God of the Bible, the God who is really there, is not only beyond the natural world but is also beyond the "supernatural" in the above limited sense. It is still appropriate to think of angels and demons and their work as supernatural, but in no way can we put these things in the same category as God and his works.

Some have suggested that we use a different word when referring to God, such as the "*supra*natural." Perhaps the word *divine* would suffice. In any case, the distinction must be clear in our minds. The ordinary and creaturely supernatural must not be confused with the divinely supernatural.

As Creator of both the visible and the invisible worlds (Colossians 1:16), God stands apart from everything else that exists. His essential being is different from that of any creature. This is what we mean when we say that God is "transcendent."

Given the fact of God's distinctness, his transcendence, his essential difference from the world, it is all the more marvelous that he should condescend to enter into this world and interact with its creatures in its ongoing history. This is exactly what he does, however. The biblical record shows how he has from the beginning revealed himself by speaking his Word to human beings, how he has appeared to certain ones in human form, how he has acted in both natural and miraculous ways to benefit mankind and save us from our sin and folly.

At the center of God's divinely supernatural deeds in this world are the Bible, Jesus Christ, and salvation. The chapters that follow will focus on aspects of these.

The Reality of God in Our Lives

In Acts 8 it is obvious that Philip and the Ethiopian eunuch assumed God's existence and his divinely supernatural intervention in their lives. The first instruction that led Philip to the eunuch was given to him by "an angel of the Lord" (v. 26). Apparently Philip accepted the fact that an angel might at any time speak a command from God to him. When Philip first saw the eunuch's chariot, the Holy Spirit continued to instruct him by speaking directly to him (v. 29). When the episode was over, the Spirit miraculously transported Philip to another place (v. 39). None of this divine activity was questioned or challenged.

As for the eunuch, he was returning home to Ethiopia after making the long journey to Jerusalem to worship Yahweh (v. 27), the God whom he knew through the Old Testament Scriptures. He apparently was a pious Jew who accepted the Scriptures as the words of God, since he was reading from Isaiah and referred to him as "the prophet" (v. 34).

The existence of God was assumed by these men because they were Bible-believing Jews. For such men the reality of Yahweh, the transcendent Creator, was the most fundamental of all beliefs. Their "golden text" was Deuteronomy 6:4, "Hear, O Israel! The Lord [Yahweh] is our God, the Lord [Yahweh] is one!" It would never have occurred to them to question this.

Outside of Judaism, however, no such assumption would be made. For example, while God's reality is only implicit in Acts 8, it is the main subject of Paul's evangelistic message in

Acts 17:22-34. Here he is not addressing Jews, but Greeks who did not know the true God. In addition to all their man-created specific deities, the Greeks in Athens dedicated one altar "to an unknown God" (v. 23), just to cover all the bases. That one "unknown God" was the true God, and Paul explained him to them.

Paul stressed first of all how the true God is the Creator and Lord of all things (v. 24) and sovereignly rules over the whole earth (v. 26). Thus he is in no way dependent on us (v. 25). We, on the other hand, are totally dependent on him (v. 28) and can find him near to us (v. 27). Because he is the sovereign Creator and we are his dependent creatures, in the end we will have to answer to him in a great day of judgment (vv. 30, 31).

It is helpful to contrast these two evangelistic situations in Acts 8 and Acts 17. They show us that where we begin in presenting the fundamentals to a seeker depends on what he or she already accepts. Most of us who have grown up in some kind of church already have a fairly solid concept of God and accept his reality.

We cannot assume that this is the case for most people who have grown up in this post-Christian world, however. Many if not most will be like the Greeks in Acts 17. They may deny God's existence outright, or they may have weak and limited ideas of God that need to be corrected.

In any case, when we presuppose nothing, we must conclude that the reality of God is the most fundamental of all truths. Why? Because if God were not *not* real, everything would change. As we have seen, there would be no absolutes, no truth. Relativism would be vindicated. This means there would be no absolutes in the area of morality—no absolute moral norms and no absolute obligation to do anything.

Also, without a Creator-God, there would be no sin and salvation. Jesus, if he existed at all, would be just a man and no more "divine" than any one of us. His life and death would have no distinctive saving power beyond that of a noble example, if we chose to accept it as such. So our Christian faith would be false and vain, and the church would be a waste of time. Judgment day, heaven, and hell would be myths.

How important it is to keep the reality of God in our minds at all times! This includes the reality of God as Trinity. Yahweh of the Old Testament is not just God the Father, but God the Son and God the Holy Spirit as well (Matthew 28:19). Philip accepted the reality of the Spirit of God (Acts 8:29) and of the deity of Jesus (Acts 8:37). (The deity of Jesus will be discussed in chapter 5.) In

Ephesians 4:4-6, in his list of the fundamental doctrines that unify Christians, Paul includes the Spirit (v. 4), the Lord (Jesus, v. 5), and the Father (v. 6).

How can we "practice the presence of God," as Brother Lawrence put it? How may we consciously be aware of him as the one in whom "we live and move and exist" (Acts 17:28)? First we must remember that we ourselves are creatures. God is not just another name for our own inner self or true being. God is our Creator, and we are at all times in total dependence on him.

Second, we must think of God not as some vague, impersonal force or power, but as a *personal* being who loves us and wants fellowship with us. This is the significance of the fact that we are made in his image (Genesis 1:26-28).

Third, we must remember that God is with us and around us. He is present to us personally and in his works, to bless us, protect us, and answer our prayers. We must learn to see him in the forces of nature, both in majestic elements like the stars and "rolling thunder," and in more modest things like flowers and breezes. We must learn to say with the songwriter, "In the rustling grass I hear him pass, he speaks to me everywhere."[5]

Fourth, as Christians whom he has saved from sin, we must think more often of the saving grace with which his love envelopes us and of the very presence in our lives and bodies of the divine Holy Spirit. How can we forget that God the Spirit *himself* dwells within us, specifically to empower us to live holy lives?

Finally, we can be conscious of God's presence in our lives every time we read the Bible or hear its message proclaimed. This is God himself speaking to us! These are his thoughts and words, falling upon our ears and taking root in our hearts.

---

[1] *National Geographic,* September 1985: 328.

[2] See my book, *What the Bible Says About God the Creator* (College Press, 1983).

[3] F. Copleston, *History of Philosophy,* I/ii (Doubleday Image), 150.

[4] See *SCP Journal,* issue entitled "Alien Encounters," 17: 1 and 2, 1992.

[5] Maltbie D. Babcock, "This Is My Father's World."

Fundamental #3

The Bible Is God's Word

In one sense any building's foundation is its most important part. It supports everything else related to the building. Thus we feel happy and secure when our house or school or church is resting on a good foundation.

Jesus talks about the proper foundation for our lives in his familiar parable of the wise and foolish builders (Matthew 7:24-27). He says that his spoken words are like a foundation of solid rock. A life built upon his words will not fall.

Ephesians 2:20 says that the church is "built upon the foundation of the apostles and prophets." In what sense can the church be built upon apostles and prophets? Ephesians 3:5 shows us the answer: *God's Word,* revealed to them through the Spirit, forms a foundation for the church.

The Divine Origin of the Bible

The fundamental importance of the words of Christ, and the words of God in general, leads us to ask these questions: Where do we find these words today? Do we have any sure access to these holy and life-giving words?

The answer is yes—the very words of God are present to us today in the form of the Bible. This is the third fundamental: *the Bible is God's Word.*

A Fundamental From the Beginning

We have seen that the basic assumption of classical liberalism was its denial of the transcendent, supernatural God. Its most open and obvious attack, however, was on the nature and truth of the Bible. It rejected the view held by Jews and then Christians for more than three thousand years—that God speaks to his people, and his divine message is preserved for the ages in the biblical writings.

Thus for liberalism the Bible was not a unique book; it was not seen as qualitatively different from all other books. It is merely a collection of human speculations about religion, the record of one group's search for God.

In eighteenth-century Europe a number of writers had already begun to attack the divine origin of Scripture in the name of higher biblical criticism. Nineteenth-century critics focused on the first five books of the Bible, traditionally held to be written by Moses by the inspiration of the Holy Spirit. The critics divided these "five books of Moses" among at least four anonymous writers and editors, labeled simply *J, E, D,* and *P.*

The critics saw the Bible as having come into existence in the same manner as all other books, with a purely human authorship. Since the various books of the Bible originated over a period of many centuries, they reflect an evolutionary development of the idea of God and religion. The earliest Hebrew documents have a rather crude idea of a barbaric sort of God. But as the centuries went by, the Jews' notion of God got more "civilized." When Jesus came along, this development reached its peak. His view of God and religion was the world's best up to that time, and is still valuable.

Of course, for liberals nothing in the Bible, not even what Jesus thought, is absolute and final. Since we are nearly two thousand years beyond Jesus, we must obviously assume that modern ideas are even nearer to the truth than those of Jesus himself.

What was happening within liberalism was that final authority was being shifted from God to man, from the Bible to human reason and experience. Recognizing human finitude, however, liberalism resigned itself to relativism. No human conclusions can ever be final; man's reason can never achieve ultimate truth. Our greatest glory and happiness come not from having and knowing the truth, but from searching for it.

In the midst of this growing tide of unbelief, those who came to be called "fundamentalists" arose in defense of the traditional belief in the divine origin of the Bible. As Millard Erickson has well expressed it, one of their unyielding doctrinal essentials was "the belief that the Holy Spirit had so influenced the writers of the Bible that their writings were not merely their words, but the very words of God, and thus completely free from error"[1]

From the beginning of this battle, the fundamentalists stressed the divine inspiration and inerrant authority of the Bible. Many Bible and prophetic conferences were held in the last quarter of the nineteenth century, always issuing in a ringing affirmation of biblical inspiration. The famous series of booklets called *The Fundamentals,* produced between 1910 and 1915, "met the liberal challenge head on. The Bible *was* the inspired word of God. It was historically accurate and . . . was totally and authoritatively reliable in presenting the way of salvation"[2]

This is the legacy inherited by modern evangelicalism. At one of the earliest evangelical conventions (in Chicago in 1943), the unanimously adopted statement of faith began with this assertion: "We believe the Bible to be the inspired, the only infallible, authoritative word of God."

This, of course, was not some new way of looking at the Bible. This is how God's people have always viewed the biblical writings. Though it was not explicitly stated in Acts 8, we can safely say that it was assumed by the eunuch as he sat in his chariot reading the prophet Isaiah (v. 28), and by Philip himself when he "opened his mouth, and beginning from this Scripture he preached Jesus to him" (v. 35).

Meaning and Implications

What do we mean when we speak of the "divine origin" of the Bible? We are referring first of all to the *process* by which the books of the Bible originated, and second to the unique nature of the *product* of this process.

• **The Process.** Two divine activities were involved in the process by which the Bible was produced. One is called *revelation.* Most people who believe in God believe also that he has revealed himself to human beings in some way or another. For some, his revealing work is limited to the various ways that he acts in the world. Certain events are taken to be God's own direct actions within human history, and by reflecting on these events we can draw important conclusions about his nature and purposes.

As an analogy, small children take the presence of gifts under the Christmas tree as a sure sign that Santa Claus has visited their house, that they have been good, and that Santa likes them and is kind to them. In a similar way, more perceptive adults observe that certain historical events (such as the deliverance of the Jews from Egypt or the crucifixion of Jesus) are the sure sign of God's presence and goodness and grace within them. Thus such events are taken as a source of revelation.

This approach to revelation is satisfactory as long as it is not seen as the only way in which God gives us revelation. Fundamental to our view of the divine origin of the Bible, and assumed throughout the Bible itself, is the fact that God not only *acts* within the world but that he also *speaks* to his people in human words and language.

In fact, that God has revealed himself in human words is one of the plainest teachings in the Bible. The Old Testament prophets constantly introduced their messages with words such as "Thus says the Lord" (Amos 1:3, 6, 9, 11, 13). Isaiah began his prophecy with the words, "Listen, O heavens, and hear, O earth; for the Lord speaks. . . . Hear the word of the Lord" (1:2, 10). David declared, "The Spirit of the Lord spoke by me, and His word was on my tongue" (2 Samuel 23:2). In Romans 3:2 the Old Testament Scriptures are called "the oracles of God," or "the very words of God" *(New International Version)*. Since Jesus himself was God incarnate (see chapter 5), every word he spoke while on earth was divine revelation. Even after he returned to the Father, he continued to speak through the Holy Spirit to and through his appointed apostles and prophets (John 16:13-15; Ephesians 3:5). Truly, as Hebrews 1:1, 2 declares, God has spoken.

Not only has he spoken, he has arranged for his revealed message to be recorded in written form in what we now call *Scripture* or *the Bible*. The agents he employed for this task were prophets and apostles who, of course, were finite human beings and thus prone to errors and lapses of memory. Now, we might think that the writing of Scripture was too important and crucial a task to entrust to mere human beings. What if they got the message mixed up, or forgot something, or added something that was not consistent with God's thoughts?

All these things were possible, of course. That is why the process by which Scripture originated involved not only revelation but also *inspiration*. God knew his human messengers were liable to err, so the Holy Spirit was appointed to oversee the actual writing of the Bible. The Spirit actively worked in the minds and hearts of the writers, giving them infallible memories and guarding their statements to guarantee their accuracy.

For example, Jesus assures us that when David wrote his Psalms, he spoke in or through the Spirit (Matthew 22:43; see Acts 28:25). The prophets spoke from God as they were "moved by the Holy Spirit," says 2 Peter 1:21. Jesus promised that his apostles would be guided by the Spirit when they taught about him (John 14:26; 16:13). Thus every word of Scripture has been "inspired by God" or breathed out by God (2 Timothy 3:16; see the *New International Version*).

This does not mean that every word of the Bible has been *revealed* by God, however. Much if not most of Scripture does consist of the divinely inspired record of divine revelation, but a good deal of what is recorded did not have to be revealed. Some was known to the writers from historical records and traditions (see Matthew 1:1-16). Some was known to them from their own research (see Luke 1:3, 4), their own experience (see 2 Corinthians 11:22-27), or their own thoughts (see 2 Timothy 4:13).

The key point is this: Though not everything in the Bible is revealed, it is all *inspired*. That is, the Holy Spirit guarded the writing not only of the revealed portions of Scripture but also of the nonrevealed portions. *All* Scripture is inspired by God (2 Timothy 3:16). Everything it says has God's "seal of approval."

• **The Product.** Given the revelation and inspiration involved in the process by which Scripture was produced, what is the nature of the product? It may be described in three ways.

First, the Bible is the *Word of God*. The "Word" or *Logos* was one of the titles applied to Jesus (John 1:1). "His name is called The Word of God" (Revelation 19:13). We must not overlook the fact, though, that the inspired words spoken through apostles and prophets are also called the Word of God. If all Scripture is literally "God-breathed" (2 Timothy 3:16, NIV), how can it be anything less than his Word?

Jesus calls certain Old Testament texts "the word of God" (Mark 7:13). Romans 3:2 speaks of the Old Testament writings in general as "the oracles *[ta logia]* of God," which literally means "the very words of God" (NIV). Paul is conscious of the fact that his inspired words are "taught by the Spirit" (1 Corinthians 2:13; see 14:37). Thus he says his message is not "the word of men" but "the word of God" (1 Thessalonians 2:13).

This is an awesome thought: When we pick up a Bible and read it, the words are in a real sense God's own words spoken from his mind into our minds. This applies even to translations of the Bible, insofar as they faithfully represent the wording and message of the original text.

Second, the Bible is *infallible* and *inerrant*. That the Bible is infallible means it is "incapable of error." This is a necessary inference from the fact that it is God's own Word. Since God knows all things (1 John 3:20), he cannot make a mistake, and since he cannot lie (Titus 1:2), he cannot deceive us. Thus anything that can truly be called "the Word of God" must be true: "Thy word is truth" (John 17:17). This is why Jesus states as a general principle that "Scripture cannot be broken" (John 10:35).

Since the Bible is infallible (incapable of error), then it must also be inerrant, which simply means "free from error." This applies specifically to the original writings as they came directly from the inspired apostles and prophets. Today we do not have the physical manuscripts produced by these writers, but we do have the original text that was on these manuscripts, since it has been ascertained with reasonable certainty by the science of textual criticism, except in a relatively few places.

This is another awesome thought: When we read the Bible, we know we are reading truth. This cannot be said of any other book. Ancient writers such as Augustine have given this advice to those who think they have found something erroneous in the Bible: Either the manuscript (or reconstructed text) is faulty, or the translator has not got the proper sense of it, or you yourself have misunderstood what the writer is saying.

Third, the Bible as the product of divine revelation and inspiration is *our one true and final authority*. This means that it has a rightful claim upon our minds and our lives. Whatever it says, we ought to believe. Whatever it commands, we ought to do. It is our God-given norm, our only rule for faith and practice. To ignore it is foolish and, in the end, fatal. (See Luke 6:46-49.)

Why Do We Believe This?

It is appropriate to ask why we should believe all these things about the Bible. Specifically, why should we believe it is the inspired and inerrant Word of God? We note first of all that it *claims* to be this, as the aforementioned Scripture references show. Just claiming it does not make it so, of course. The reason why we believe it is that the relevant evidence proves it to be so.

In this short chapter we cannot set forth all the arguments or evidences that support the Bible's claim to be the Word of God. Refer to a volume such as Josh McDowell's *Evidence That Demands a Verdict* for a competent survey.

The one thing to be mentioned here is the evidence from fulfilled prophecy. Old Testament prophecies about Jesus especially, such as the one being read by the eunuch when Philip came to him, are proof the Bible is from God. Only God could know the future with such precision that he could confidently prophesy the details of the life of Christ from his birth (Micah 5:2) to his death (Psalm 22:11-18). The only reasonable explanation for fulfilled prophecy and other such facts about the Bible is that it is indeed what it claims to be: the Word of God.

Why Is This Fundamental?

The first three essentials—that truth itself is fundamental, that God is real, and that the Bible is God's Word—are inseparably linked. First, truth is necessary if we hope to avoid relativism with its ensuing social, moral, and personal chaos. Second, an infinite, omniscient Creator-God is necessary as the only source of such truth. Finally, for this truth to be available to us, it is necessary for God to speak to us in language we can understand. This takes place in and through the Bible.

This is why it is essential that we see the Bible as the Word of God. Even if an omniscient God exists, unless we have some kind of communication from him, human beings still have no access to absolute truth. We are still locked in relativism.

This is the reason that revelation is necessary. Revelation is the basic means by which God communicates his sure and certain knowledge to us. He unveils the very contents of his own mind, providing us with truth (John 17:17). Through inspiration God's appointed messengers have inerrantly recorded this revealed truth, along with other relevant truth, in the pages of Scripture. Because the Bible is God's Word, we have sure and certain truth.

Without the Bible, we would be adrift in a dangerous sea of doubt and uncertainty, without a map or compass.

Some may say that we should not consider this to be an essential because it tends to draw our attention away from the one true essential, Jesus Christ. They may say that all we really need is a knowledge of Jesus, specifically a knowledge of the historical events that are included in "the gospel": that Christ died for our sins, that he was buried, and that he was raised on the third day (1 Corinthians 15:1-4).

These facts of the gospel are indeed essential and central in their own way, to be sure. Also, the basic historical data about Jesus—that he lived, that he was crucified, that he arose from the dead—may be established from the biblical writings through ordinary historical investigation, without any necessary acknowledgement that they are the Word of God.

But this in itself is not enough. Ordinary historical study may show us that these important events actually took place, but without revelation from God we could never discover their true meaning. First Corinthians 15:3 says not only that "Christ died," a historical event, but also that he died "for our sins," the meaning of the event. The latter is a revealed truth.

But even this simple statement is not the whole story. What does it mean to say that Christ died for our sins? Exactly how was his death "for our sins"? To answer this we need even further revelation, such as that provided in the text from which the eunuch was reading, a section we know today as part of Isaiah 53. From this and other key texts (such as Romans 3:23-26) we learn the truth about how Christ's death saves us from our sins.

So inspired Scripture is necessary for the preaching of the gospel. From it alone we learn both the historical facts of the gospel and the meaning of those facts. Paul's full statement in 1 Corinthians 15:3 is "that Christ died for our sins according to the Scriptures." That "Christ died" is the essential fact; that he died "for our sins" is the essential meaning; "according to the Scriptures" identifies the essential source of these truths.

That is why Scripture can be called the foundation on which the church is built. This is the meaning of Ephesians 2:20, where Paul says the church is "built upon the foundation of the apostles and prophets." The only way apostles and prophets can be such a foundation is through their teaching; the only sure source of their teaching available to us today is the Bible. The church today continues to be built on the foundation of this Book.

Some may object that Jesus is supposed to be "the church's one foundation," citing Matthew 16:16-18 and 1 Corinthians 3:11. It is true that Jesus and his work are in a sense the metaphysical foundation of the church. That is, the reality of Jesus and his work are the basis for the reality of the church. The Bible can never take the place of Jesus as this kind of foundation.

Rather, the inspired Word of God is what may be called the epistemological foundation of the church. That is, it is the only basis for our *knowledge* about Christ and his work. Christ and his work would be in vain unless there were some sure way to know about it. The Bible is essential for this purpose.

Each of us must ask himself this question: Am I truly basing my beliefs, my values, and my life on the teachings of God's Word? If not Scripture, what? Remember that "all other ground is sinking sand," as Matthew 7:24-27 and Luke 6:46-49 indicate.

The Clarity of Scripture

Many people think of the Bible as some dark, mysterious, obscure book that can be understood only by mystical or monkish types that spend every waking moment poring over it. This is not the case. The Bible *can* be understood by ordinary people.

But isn't the Bible the Word of *God?* Surely any message spoken by the omnipotent, omniscient God must be beyond anything us poor, puny mortals can understand. If (as some think) even a human Ph.D. must always speak over everyone's head, how can we be expected to comprehend anything *God* says?

Actually, this is carrying the argument in the wrong direction. It is unfortunately true that human scholars are often guilty of "obfuscation" (speaking in dark, confusing, bewildering, obscure language!). But that is not because they are "too smart" for us ordinary people; rather, it is because they are not smart enough, at least in the art of communication. I have observed that the more a person knows about any given subject, the more clearly he will be able to explain it to his intended audience.

If this is true (and I believe it is), then God's omniscience will not be a hindrance to communication with us creatures, but will actually facilitate it. This is the assumption with which we should approach the Bible. If it is truly God's Word, then it is necessarily something we *can* understand.

Several points need to be distinguished and stressed here. First, every statement in the Bible has a specific, intended meaning. When first spoken by their authors, the statements of Scripture were not just words or sounds. They meant something.

It is surprising how many people today deny this. It is common to hear or read some variation of this idea: "There is no one right interpretation of Scripture."

We need to think this through. If biblical statements have no specifically intended meanings, then there is still no real communication from God. If we approach the Bible assuming that it can have various meanings for different people, then each person is free to use the Bible just to reinforce his own ideas. Absolute truth is still absent; relativism still reigns. As far as truth is concerned, we are still no better off than if God had not communicated with us, or even if there were no God at all. "One interpretation is as good as another" in the end means that "one Bible (Christian, Hindu, Mormon) is as good as another."

The second point is that God *intends* for us to understand his Word. Why else would he have given it to us? When he approached the eunuch, who was reading Scripture (Isaiah 53), Philip asked him, "Do you understand what you are reading?" (Acts 8:30). Philip did not say, "Beats me! I don't understand it either!" Instead, he began at that very Scripture and explained Jesus to the man.

Jesus said, "You shall know the truth, and the truth shall make you free" (John 8:32). To *know* the truth means not just to be able to identify it or to know how to pronounce its words. It also means to *understand* it. This is Jesus' intention for us.

The third point is that we *can* understand God's Word. Some have taught that sinners cannot truly understand the Bible because sin has clouded their minds and short-circuited their reasoning processes. This is part of the doctrine known as total depravity. It is then inferred that God (specifically the Holy Spirit) must uncloud a person's mind and disclose the right understanding of Scripture to him in an act of "illumination."

Scripture does not teach the doctrine of total depravity, however. Nor does it teach that our innate reasoning ability is directly impaired by sin. God directs his Word not just to believers but also to sinners. He appeals to sinners to use their powers of reason: "'Come now, and let us reason together,' says the Lord, 'Though your sins are as scarlet, they will be as white as snow'" (Isaiah 1:18). His Word is written so that sinners can understand it and come to faith in Jesus: "These have been written that you may believe that Jesus is the Christ, the Son of God; and that believing you may have life in His name" (John 20:31).

If even sinners can understand God's Word, then surely a believer can. If we cannot, then either God is mocking us in texts such as the above or he does not know how to communicate with us. Neither conclusion is acceptable.

This leads to some very serious questions. If we truly *can* understand the Bible, why do we seem to have so much difficulty doing so? Also, why do sincere people understand it differently? Finally, how can we have any kind of certainty about our own particular interpretations and convictions? Here are three considerations to help us in answering these questions.

First, Scripture must be studied holistically. That is, each part of the Bible must be understood in light of its overall teaching on any particular subject. The Bible may be clear, but it is not necessarily simple. All parts are not equally understandable. A basic rule of interpretation is that the less clear must be seen in the light of the more clear.

Does this mean that everyone must remain agnostic or skeptical as to the meaning of any Bible text until he has spent years studying it all? The answer is no. Here is where the role of human teachers comes in. When Philip asked the eunuch if he understood what he was reading, the eunuch replied, "Well, how could I, unless someone guides me?" (Acts 8:31). Philip then assumed the role of the teacher, and explained Isaiah 53:7, 8 to him.

This illustrates a main difference between teacher and student in the process of Bible study. The eunuch did not understand the text because he did not yet have the whole picture of God's revelation. He did not know Jesus Christ and the New Covenant. On the other hand, Philip did have this whole picture.

Likewise, today we can be more sure of our understanding of the Bible when we have studied it holistically, either on our own or at the feet of a teacher who has already done so.

Second, personal experiences must be interpreted by the Bible, not vice versa. Like Philip and the eunuch, we must begin with Scripture (Acts 8:35) and let our experiences conform to what it says. We fall into grievous error when we base our conclusions about biblical truth on personal experience. Compare Matthew 7:21-23, where experience is the foundation, with Matthew 7:24-27, where the Word is the foundation.

Third, the real barrier to true biblical understanding is not a sin-clouded intellect but a sin-hardened will. The problem is not inability to see the truth, but unwillingness to accept the truth. This unwillingness may be due to a desire to protect a sinful habit or lifestyle, a reluctance to admit previous error, or an emotional or financial commitment to some denominational tradition. Whatever the reason, it is true that our sin causes us to "suppress the truth in unrighteousness" (Romans 1:18; see 1:18-32). Ignorance and darkened understanding are too often rooted in hardness of heart (Ephesians 4:18).

We cannot be sure that we are understanding the Bible correctly until in our hearts we have put everything on the line, until we are willing to risk everything—pride, family, friends, job, pension—in our quest for true understanding of God's Word. The Holy Spirit's proper role in this process is to give us the moral power to subordinate our wills to the clear Word of God.

Knowing the intended meaning of a statement from God is as essential for truth as knowing the statement itself. This does not mean we will ever know everything meant or implied by any given statement; it means only that we must know its basic meaning. This is essential for truth and sound doctrine, and it is especially important as we consider the subjects in the following chapters.

---

[1] *The New Evangelical Theology* (Revell 1968), 22.

[2] John D. Woodbridge et al., *The Gospel in America: Themes in the Story of America's Evangelicals* (Grand Rapids: Zondervan 1979), 58.

Fundamental #4

Jesus Is Our Savior

The first three essentials are the basic framework of our faith: truth itself is fundamental, God is real, the Bible is God's Word. In their barest form, these essentials do not include anything that is explicitly and distinctively Christian. They are rather the pre-requisites of our specifically Christian faith.

The last four essentials, however, *are* distinctively Christian. They are the essence of Christian faith, the core of what it means to be a Christian. They all refer to Jesus Christ and to the salvation he has brought to the human race.

The Bible does not record the content of Philip's sermon to the Ethiopian eunuch in Acts 8. It simply says he "preached Jesus to him" (v. 35). As a pious Jew, the eunuch already believed in God and in the Old Testament Scriptures as God's Word of truth. These points did not have to be emphasized. What he did not yet know was the gospel of Jesus Christ; this is what Philip taught him.

Even in proclaiming the gospel, some facts take priority over others. Of "first importance," says Paul, are these things: "that Christ died for our sins according to the Scriptures, and that He was buried, and that He was raised on the third day according to the Scriptures" (1 Corinthians 15:1-4). Because he did these things, *Jesus is our Savior.* This is the fourth fundamental.

Jesus Is the Christ

When a sinner first begins to believe in Jesus, a common practice is to ask him to confess his faith, using the words of Peter in Matthew 16:16, "Thou art the Christ, the Son of the living God." So the first thing many of us affirmed about Jesus was that he is the Christ. To Christians he is and always will be the Christ.

It may be fair to ask, though, whether we really knew what we were asserting when we mouthed the words, "Jesus is the Christ." If Philip had been there, he might have inquired of us, "Do you understand what you are saying?" He might ask the same question of us even after we have been Christians awhile. We still constantly refer to Jesus as "the Christ." What does this mean?

Sometimes we may think of it just as part of Jesus' full name: "John Jones, meet Jesus Christ." It is not improper to use the term as part of Jesus' name, but it is more than that. It is a kind of title, a title that embodies the fullness of Jesus' mission on earth.

Exactly what does this title mean? What are we saying when we confess Jesus to be "the Christ"? More to the point, what did Peter have in mind when he applied this word to Jesus? What would any good first-century Jew have meant by this?

Our English word *Christ* comes directly from the Greek term *christos,* which is a translation of the Hebrew term *mashiach* (from which we get our English word *Messiah).* Both the Greek and the Hebrew words mean "the anointed one." So when we confess Jesus is the Christ, we are confessing him to be the anointed one.

But what is the significance of this? Again we must ask what a first-century Jew would mean by calling someone "the anointed one." The answer lies in the Old Testament practice of anointing. Literally it was the pouring of oil (such as olive oil) on a person's head. In the history of Israel this was like an ordination service that conferred God's blessing on the person chosen to fill an office of leadership. Those ascending to the office of king were anointed (David, 1 Samuel 16:3, 12, 13), as were those who became high priests (Aaron, Exodus 29:7; see 29:29), and at least one prophet (Elisha, 1 Kings 19:16).

In conjunction with this familiar practice of anointing, God began to reveal through the prophets his plan to send a great King and High Priest (see Psalm 110) who would be Israel's deliverer and the universal ruler and savior of all mankind. He would be the "Messiah" (see Psalm 2:2), the one *anointed* to work this work of salvation in fulfillment of these prophecies. Pious Jews thus were filled with a great hope for and expectation of this anointed one, this Messiah, this Christ.

So when Peter said of Jesus, "Thou art the Christ," he was identifying him as the long-awaited, divinely sent Savior. Although at that point he did not yet understand *how* Jesus would work his work of salvation (see Matthew 16:21-23), Peter knew that Jesus was indeed the one anointed by God to save the world.

Likewise, when we confess "Jesus is the Christ," we are acknowledging him as our only Savior and are declaring that this will be our relationship to him from this point forward. We are affirming the truth of Paul's statement, "that Christ Jesus came into the world to save sinners" (1 Timothy 1:15).

It is not enough to relate to Jesus just as the incarnation and model of true godhood among us. Nor is it enough to look to him simply as the model of a perfect human life. He cannot be to us just a teacher of proper values, or an inspiring leader, or a friend to quell our loneliness. He is indeed all of these things, but none of them is the essential aspect of his messiahship. What is essential and most important is that he is our *Savior.* This is how we must think of him and relate to him first of all.

Christ Died for Our Sins

As soon as Peter confessed Jesus as the Christ, Jesus began to teach his disciples that as the Christ he must be put to death and be raised from the dead on the third day (Matthew 16:21). At first they could not understand this (v. 22), but ultimately it became clear that Christ's death and resurrection are the two primary pillars of his saving work. They are the chief elements of the gospel (1 Corinthians 15:1-4).

Thus Christians have always affirmed that one fundamental doctrine of our faith is that "Christ died for our sins." To deny this is to deny Christianity. Therefore it is essential that we believe it, and also that we understand what it means.

Sin and Its Punishment

To say that "Christ died for our sins" presupposes the idea that mankind's basic problem is sin. This cannot be taken for granted.

When we look outside the biblical revelation, in pagan religions and philosophical speculations, there is no real concept of man as sinner. Instead, man's basic problem is identified as either ignorance or weakness, or a combination of both.

For example, Hinduism says all human suffering can be traced to each individual's ignorance of his own true self. Christian liberalism says that what is often called sin is just an innate spiritual weakness because human beings have not yet evolved very far beyond the animal stage. So they are still vulnerable to the old animal instincts of violence and selfishness and greed in the interests of self-preservation.

Obviously, if mankind's problem is basically ignorance or some form of weakness, then the solution will be either knowledge or empowerment. A "savior" will be someone who can enlighten us and dispel our ignorance, or someone who can inspire and motivate us to conquer our baser instincts.

It is certainly true that lost human beings are ignorant and weak, and that they need knowledge and power. But this is not our basic problem. The Bible says that our root problem is sin. Christ died not for our ignorance, not for our weakness, but for our sins (1 Corinthians 15:3). Christ Jesus came into the world to save sinners (1 Timothy 1:15), not to teach the ignorant and to empower the weak.

How one understands the human predicament is directly connected to whether he believes in God, and to whether he sees God as the absolute Creator of all things. In any world view without the transcendent Creator-God, there can be no true concept of sin. Sin is transgression of law (1 John 3:4), and only the Creator has an inherent right to issue laws that are binding on his creatures. Since the concept of *ex nihilo* creation is virtually unknown outside the Bible, it is no surprise that nonbiblical world views do not contain a true concept of sin.

The biblical God, though, is the absolute Creator and so the owner of all things (Psalm 24:1, 2). He gives us laws (James 4:12) that we are absolutely obligated to obey. Disobedience and rebellion against his laws are the essence of sin (1 John 3:4).

Understanding sin as a violation of God's law means that not only sin but also salvation itself will be permeated with legal ramifications and connotations. The logical result of sin is guilt, and the necessary consequence of guilt is punishment. In the Bible the punishment for sin is summed up as death: "The wages of sin is death" (Romans 6:23). This includes not only physical death, the death of the body (Romans 8:10), but also the state of eternal death, a complete separation from God and his goodness (2 Thessalonians 1:9; Revelation 20:14). This separation from God is what we call *hell*.

Law, sin, guilt, judgment, wrath, punishment, death, hell—these are all part of a single package. Law does not have to be broken, of course. But once sin has entered the picture, none of the elements in this list can be set aside. This is basically because the Creator and Lawgiver is a *holy* God. Since his holiness is part of his nature, and since he must be true to his own nature, once sin has been committed, it *must* be punished. By his very nature "our God is a consuming fire" (Hebrews 12:29); the fire of his wrath *must* be poured out on the sinner.

Mankind's sinful predicament is daunting indeed. One could not imagine a worse situation from which we need to be saved. And yet, in the face of what seems to be an impossible challenge, "Christ Jesus came into the world to save sinners."

The Substitutionary Atonement

Since God is a consuming fire of wrath, why does he not just immediately send sinners to hell? Because his nature consists not only of holy wrath, but also of loving grace. While his holiness requires him to punish sinners, his grace causes him to desire to save them at whatever cost to himself.

Thus God's response to sin includes condemnation, to be sure, but it also includes a great and marvelous plan to save sinners from their deserved punishment. At the heart of this saving plan is Christ's death on the cross.

• **Inadequate Interpretations of the Cross.** We have said that an essential truth includes not only the bare statement of that truth but also the intended meaning of that statement. What is the meaning of "Christ died for our sins"? Not all Christians have agreed on this, and some interpretations of the cross have been seriously inadequate. That is, they do not explain how the cross saves sinners from their sin.

A view that was popular in the first few Christian centuries was that the cross was God's way of tricking the devil into giving up his rightful claims on sinners, thus allowing them to become God's possessions once more. The assumption is that when we sin we become the legal property of Satan; he then has the right to hold onto us as his captives. Even God has to honor this right.

Thus sinners could be saved only if Satan could be persuaded to relinquish his ownership rights. But how is this possible? God's wisdom was equal to the task. God the Son, the divine *Logos*, took on a human form, disguising himself as the human being Jesus. He then went about doing marvelous things, such as raising people from the dead. This attracted the devil's attention and caused him to covet Jesus. But since Jesus committed no sin, Satan had no legal claim on him. So God struck a bargain with the devil: He would give him Jesus' life as a ransom payment in exchange for the lives of all the sinners of the world. Satan accepted the deal, and so Jesus was crucified on the cross.

The trick was that Satan did not know that Jesus was God and so could not truly be overcome by death. So when Jesus arose from the dead, he escaped Satan's grip by his sheer power. The devil is left with nothing.

This view did not have a lasting influence. Though Jesus' plan did involve the defeat of Satan, this was not how the cross fit into that plan.

A later view of the meaning of the cross says it was a way of scaring sinners into being good. Actually God can forgive sins without the cross, and he is willing to do so. The only problem is that if he begins handing out forgiveness wholesale, people might get the wrong idea about sin. They might conclude that it is not all that serious, and sin might just multiply upon the earth.

So to instill in mankind a proper sense of the heinousness of sin, God showed us what sin really deserves by pouring out his wrath on Jesus. The cross is a kind of object lesson meant to shock us and instill fear in our hearts and deter us from sinning.

This view was not widely accepted either. It is mostly speculation, and it does not do justice to the "consuming fire" nature of God that demands and requires punishment for sin.

The most popular inadequate view of the cross is called the *moral influence* theory. Like the last view, it says that God could easily forgive sins without the cross, if only he could convince sinners that he is ready and able to do so. The problem is that for one reason or another sinners just refuse to believe it and refuse to accept the offered forgiveness. So God must do something to show that he really does love the sinner, something that will break down the sinner's resistance and motivate him to turn to God in repentance and reciprocal love. The cross is designed to do just this. Via the cross God says to the sinner, "See how much I love you? Please soften your heart and come to me!"

This view is ideal for liberals and others who see man's main problem as ignorance or weakness. The cross dispels ignorance by revealing how much God love us; it overcomes our weakness by motivating us to turn to God and accept his love. Man's sin itself is not the problem directly addressed by the cross.

Though it is true that the cross does reveal God's love and motivate sinners to repent, the moral influence theory cannot explain *how* it does these things. The element of the cross that reveals God's love and melts sinners hearts is the fact of *substitution*, which is the very thing liberals reject.

• **Christ Is Our Substitute.** The last view discussed above was and is common among those who espouse the classical liberal view of Christianity. When the early fundamentalists rose up to confront liberalism, they knew that this "moral influence" theory of the cross robbed Christianity of its heart and soul. Thus they named the *substitutionary atonement* as one of the nonnegotiable fundamentals of the faith.

Scripture specifically says that "Christ died for our sins." The only view of the cross that adequately explains this fact is the reality of substitution. We as sinners deserve the punishment of physical and eternal death for our sins. But Jesus Christ chose to be our substitute—he took upon himself the penalty we deserve. He died *for* us; he died *instead* of us; he died *in our place*.

It seems to be nothing less than providential that the eunuch was reading the book of Isaiah when Philip was told to confront him (Acts 8:26-28). It is even more significant that he was reading one of the greatest prophecies of the coming Messiah. Most remarkable of all is that he was reading from the very section (our chapter 53) that teaches that the Messiah's work would be to bear the punishment for our sins in our place. When Philip began with this Scripture and "preached Jesus to him," he must have begun with the fact of the substitutionary atonement.

Here are some of the words of this great prophecy: "Surely our griefs He Himself bore, and our sorrows He carried; yet we ourselves esteemed Him stricken, smitten of God, and afflicted. But He was pierced through for our transgressions, He was crushed for our iniquities; the chastening for our well-being fell upon Him, and by His scourging we are healed. All of us like sheep have gone astray, each of us has turned to his own way; but the Lord has caused the iniquity of us all to fall on Him" (Isaiah 53:4-6). Isaiah says that "He was cut off out of the land of the living, for the transgression of my people to whom the stroke was due"

(v. 8). Also, "The Righteous One, My Servant, will justify the many, as He will bear their iniquities" (v. 11). "He Himself bore the sin of many, and interceded for the transgressors" (v. 12).

The specific words the eunuch was reading included Isaiah 53:7, cited in Acts 8:32 as, "He was led as a sheep to slaughter; and as a lamb before its shearer is silent, so He does not open His mouth." To a Jew the imagery of a sheep being slain would have unmistakably called to mind the various Old Covenant sacrifices in which a sheep or a lamb would be offered up to God. That this was the intended connection is shown by the statement in Isaiah 53:10: "But the Lord was pleased to crush Him, putting Him to grief; if He would render Himself as a guilt offering."

The Hebrew word translated "guilt offering" here is the same as that used for the guilt or trespass offerings prescribed by the Law of Moses in Leviticus 5:6–6:7. These offerings, along with the sin offerings (Leviticus 4:1-35) and the sacrifices on the Day of Atonement (Leviticus 16:1-28), involved the principle of substitution. In them the sins of the people were symbolically transferred from the sinners themselves to the innocent substitutes, who were then put to death in the place of the guilty ones.

Animals cannot literally bear the sins of people, of course. These animal sacrifices were symbolic prophecies of the one true Lamb of God, Jesus Christ, who on the cross became our literal substitute, our "guilt offering." This is clearly taught in the book of Hebrews, especially in chapters 9 and 10. Jesus was "offered once to bear the sins of many" (Hebrews 9:28).

A clear New Testament affirmation of the substitutionary atonement is the description of Jesus as a *hilasterion* in Romans 3:25 and a *hilasmos* in 1 John 2:2; 4:10. These similar words are translated as "propitiation" in the *King James Version* and *New American Standard Bible*. They are translated as "sacrifice of atonement" or "atoning sacrifice" in the *New International Version*. Their basic meaning is "an offering that turns away wrath."

In what way was Jesus a propitiation? The answer is simple. Sin draws the wrath of God like iron draws a magnet. But Christ on the cross took our sins upon himself, drawing the wrath of God away from us and upon himself. When he bore our sins, he became the object of God's wrath in our place, as our substitute.

This is also taught in 2 Corinthians 5:21, which says that God "made Him who knew no sin [Jesus] to be sin on our behalf, that we might become the righteousness of God in Him." Salvation in a real sense involves trading places with Jesus. He puts himself in our place, and God treats him as we deserve, namely, as a sinner. But then we are put in Jesus' place, and God treats us as *he* deserves, namely, as a righteous one who never sinned.

Galatians 3:13 says, "Christ redeemed us from the curse of the Law, having become a curse for us." This curse of the Law is the penalty of death. As our substitute Christ took our curse for us.

Echoing Isaiah 53, the apostle Peter says of Christ, "He Himself bore our sins in His body on the cross . . . ; for by His wounds you were healed" (1 Peter 2:24).

Here is a point that must not be missed. When Christ "bore our sins" and became a curse for us, he took upon himself the *whole* penalty for *all* the sins of the *whole* human race. This means not only that he was suffering physical death in his body, but also that he was suffering in his heart and soul the equivalent of eternal death in hell for every member of the human race.

The physical agony of crucifixion was exceedingly intense, but this was next to nothing compared to the unbelievable spiritual and emotional anguish that crushed Jesus' soul beginning in the Garden of Gethsemane. There he "began to be very distressed and troubled" and said, "My soul is deeply grieved to the point of death" (Mark 14:33, 34). As he prayed, he was "in agony," and "His sweat became like drops of blood, falling down upon the ground" (Luke 22:44). On the cross he experienced the ultimate torment of hell, the sense of separation from God (Mark 15:34).

Why should our salvation require such extreme measures? Basically because God is who he is. "God is love" and wants to save us (1 John 4:8), but he is also "a consuming fire" whose holy wrath must be satisfied (Hebrews 12:29). Through the cross God could be true to both sides of his nature, satisfying his wrath through the Substitute and saving those who believe in him (Romans 3:26).

The reality of the substitutionary atonement is truly one of the essentials of our Christian faith. It is in a sense the "bull's-eye of the bull's-eye." It is the very essence of the grace of God, which in itself makes Christianity unique.

Christ Was Raised From the Dead

Jesus' work as "the Christ" was not over when he died. He was anointed not only to fill the role of a high priest and offer himself up as an atoning sacrifice for our sins. He was anointed also to be a king, conquering his enemies and reigning in victory and dividing the spoils with his people. This he did primarily in and through his resurrection from the dead.

An essential part of the gospel is that Christ "was raised on the third day" (1 Corinthians 15:4). We must believe this in order to be saved: "If you confess with your mouth Jesus as Lord, and believe in your heart that God raised Him from the dead, you shall be saved" (Romans 10:9). In Acts 8 it is significant that Philip only *began* his preaching with Isaiah 53. Without a doubt, in addition to telling the eunuch about Christ's substitutionary death, Philip also explained the Redeemer's triumphant resurrection from the dead. This was the most common theme in the early proclamation of the gospel. (See Acts 2:24-32; 3:15; 4:10, 33; 5:30; 10:40, 41; 13:30-37; 17:3, 18, 31; 26:23.)

Some have tried to spiritualize this event, interpreting it in ways that deny the literal resurrection of Christ's body from the state of death. For example, some have said that Jesus' spirit made contact with his apostles in a kind of nonmaterial apparition. Others have said that the phrase "Jesus rose from the dead" means that *faith* in him as the Messiah *arose* in the hearts of his disciples even though he had died. Through their faith they kept his memory and his ideals alive.

Such denials of any true resurrection were typical of the classical liberalism opposed by the early fundamentalists. This is why the fundamentalists cited as a core Christian doctrine the *bodily* resurrection of Jesus. This asserts what the Bible teaches: the actual physical body of Jesus was revived or resuscitated; it was changed from death to life. Jesus came forth from the tomb in his own recognizable, touchable, flesh-and-bones, eating-and-drinking body (Luke 24:36-43; John 20:16, 17, 27; Acts 10:41).

One question remains: what was the saving significance of Christ's bodily resurrection? How was this event related to his work as our Savior? The following is a list of five ways we are saved by his resurrection.

First, Christ's resurrection demonstrates his lordship. During his earthly ministry, Jesus made many claims that seem outrageous coming from a mere carpenter of Nazareth. He claimed to be the Christ, the Son of God (Matthew 16:16-20); to be sent by God (John 8:42); to be one with the Father (John 10:30); to deserve honor equal with that given to the Father (John 5:23); to have authority to forgive sins (Matthew 9:2-6); to be king (John

18:37) and Lord (Luke 6:46); to be Lord of the temple (John 2:14-22), Lord of the Sabbath (Matthew 12:8), and Lord of angels (Matthew 24:31).

All these claims were put on the line when Jesus was put to death. But when God raised him from the dead, they were shown to be true. Jesus was indeed who he claimed to be. He was "declared the Son of God with power by the resurrection from the dead" (Romans 1:4). The risen Christ declared that he had been given all authority in heaven and on earth (Matthew 28:18). By raising him from the dead and inviting him to sit at his own right hand, the Father demonstrated Jesus' lordship to the whole world (Acts 2:32-36).

Second, Christ's resurrection devastates his enemies. One purpose for his incarnation was to confront death and Satan head-on and to utterly defeat and destroy them. He came "that He might destroy the works of the devil" (1 John 3:8; see Hebrews 2:14, 15). His resurrection was a victory over these enemies. On the cross the serpent bruised his heel, but in his resurrection Jesus crushed the serpent's head (Genesis 3:15). He broke the power of death (Acts 2:24). "I was dead," says the risen Christ, but "behold, I am alive forevermore, and I have the keys of death and of Hades" (Revelation 1:18). He shares this victory with us.

Third, Christ's resurrection inaugurates the kingdom. The Old Testament foretold that the great king would come and establish his eternal kingdom (Daniel 2:44). Jesus was that king, and his very presence made the kingdom near (Matthew 3:2; 12:28). By virtue of his resurrection, he was enthroned as king at God's own right hand (Acts 2:34-36; 1 Corinthians 15:25; Matthew 26:64), where he reigns as King of Kings and Lord of Lords (Revelation 19:16).

Fourth, Christ's resurrection validates the cross. His death was a defeat for his enemies (Hebrews 2:14, 15; Colossians 2:15), But this did not become obvious until the resurrection. His enemies thought they had beaten him through the cross (1 Corinthians 2:8); but when he arose, they realized it was the other way around. Satan cannot automatically drag us down with him to eternal death merely by luring us into sin. The cross has paid that penalty of eternal death for us, and the risen Christ is enthroned at God's right hand as the constant reminder that the price for our sins has been paid (Hebrews 4:14-16; 7:25; 8:1). "Christ Jesus is He who died, yes, rather who was raised, who is at the right hand of God, who also intercedes for us" (Romans 8:34).

Fifth, Christ's resurrection invigorates the dead. When he personally burst the bonds of death, he unleashed renewing, life-giving power that will ultimately envelop the universe, producing new heavens and a new earth (2 Peter 3:13). As the first fruits of the new creation, he is the source and guarantee of a more abundant harvest (1 Corinthians 15:20, 21).

As believers, we are part of that harvest, and the power of his resurrection is already at work in us (Ephesians 1:18-20). It began when our dead souls received new life in Christian baptism (Romans 6:3, 4), when we were "raised up with Him" (Colossians 2:12) and saved "through the resurrection of Jesus" (1 Peter 3:21). This resurrection power is with us to the end, when the same Spirit who raised up Jesus will give us new bodies on the last day (Romans 8:11). Thus we are not afraid of death, because we have "a living hope through the resurrection of Jesus Christ" (1 Peter 1:3).

This fourth fundamental—Jesus is our Savior—is well summed up in Romans 5:10: "For if while we were enemies, we were reconciled to God through the death of His Son, much more, having been reconciled, we shall be saved by His life." These are absolutely essential. Apart from the cross, there is no other sacrifice for sins (Hebrews 10:26). And if Christ did not rise from the dead, our faith is vain and we are still in our sins (1 Corinthians 15:14, 17).

But to the eternal praise of God's grace and to our everlasting gratitude, the substitutionary atonement is real, and Christ's bodily resurrection is *real*. HALLELUJAH!

Fundamental #5

Jesus Is God's Son

"And Philip . . . preached Jesus to him" (Acts 8:35). Without any doubt the main subject of this message was the saving work of Jesus. It is reasonable to ask, though, whether Philip would have said anything to the eunuch about who Jesus is. What kind of person must the Savior be, to be able to accomplish "so great a salvation" (Hebrews 2:3).

Who did Jesus' earliest followers believe him to be? Who was he in the eyes of his apostles and other contemporaries? What did the first Christians believe? What does the Bible teach about Jesus' nature and person?

Jesus' first disciples and the first Christians had something in common: they were all Jews. Thus their understanding of the identity of Jesus was based largely on the Old Testament and its prophecies of the coming Messiah.

These prophecies include two distinct strands. First, it was foretold that "a Redeemer will come to Zion" to save his people (Isaiah 59:20). The Redeemer describes his work like this: "The Lord has anointed me to bring good news to the afflicted; He has sent me to bind up the brokenhearted, to proclaim liberty to captives, and freedom to prisoners; to proclaim the favorable year of the Lord" (Isaiah 61:1, 2; see Luke 4:17-21).

Second, the Old Testament foretold that God himself would

personally come to save his people. "'Comfort, O comfort My people,' says your God. . . . A voice is calling, 'Clear the way for the Lord in the wilderness; make smooth in the desert a highway for our God'" (Isaiah 40:1, 3). "'Behold, I am going to send My messenger, and he will clear the way before Me. And the Lord, whom you seek, will suddenly come to His temple . . . ,' says the Lord of hosts" (Malachi 3:1).

These two strands of prophecy were brought together in Jesus of Nazareth. Not only was he the Christ, the one anointed to save, he was also the Son of God, the divine Lord himself.

The Divine Nature of Jesus

The Bible shows that Jesus was not just a man with a fully *human* nature. He surely was this, but he was more. He was also God with a fully *divine* nature. This is clearly seen in several ways.

The Titles of Jesus

Whereas the title "Christ" refers especially to the work of Jesus, three other titles affirm his divine nature. The first of these is "the Son of God." Jesus himself once asked the Pharisees, "What do you think about the Christ, whose son is He?" (Matthew 22:42). Jesus had already declared that Peter's answer to this question is the correct one: "Thou art the Christ, the Son of the living God" (Matthew 16:16, 17).

This title is used in several senses in Scripture. It is applied to Israel (Hosea 11:1), to angels (Job 1:6; 2:1; 38:7), and to Christians (Romans 8:14, 19). In the pagan world it was a common title for deities. The crucial question, however, is what connotation Jesus' Jewish contemporaries attached to it. This will show us exactly what Peter was confessing in Matthew 16:16, and it will tell us how to understand the other thirty or so times the title was applied to Jesus.

Jesus clearly knew himself to be the Son of God in a unique sense. He told us to address God as "our Father" (Matthew 6:9), but many times he called God "my Father" in a way that set him apart from the rest of us. After healing a man on the Sabbath day he declared, "My Father is working until now, and I Myself am working" (John 5:17), In the ensuing discussion he emphasized this relationship over and over (John 5:17-43).

On another occasion he did the same thing. When the hostile Jews challenged him to identify himself, Jesus referred to God as "my Father" (John 10:25, 29, 37). This was the same as saying, "I am the Son of God" (v. 36). And in this connection he pointedly affirmed, "I and the Father are one" (v. 30).

At his trial, when asked whether he was the Son of God (Matthew 26:63; Mark 14:61), Jesus answered, "I am" (Mark 14:62).

The significance of this is how Jesus' enemies reacted to his claims to be God's Son: they sought to kill him, because he "was calling God His own Father, making Himself equal with God" (John 5:18). Invoking the Old Testament law against blasphemy (Leviticus 24:16), they planned to stone him—"because You, being a man, make Yourself out to be God" (John 10:31-33). Jesus ought to die, they said, "because He made Himself out to be the Son of God" (John 19:7).

Even more significant is the fact that Jesus never denied this implication of calling himself the Son of God. It was indeed a claim to deity.

The early Christians continued to preach Jesus as the Son of God. Peter had already identified him thus prior to Pentecost (Matthew 16:16). As soon as Saul (Paul) was converted, "he began to proclaim Jesus in the synagogues, saying, 'He is the Son of God'" (Acts 9:20). He was no doubt echoing the common message of early Christian evangelists. One manuscript tradition of Acts has the eunuch making this confession in 8:37: "I believe that Jesus Christ is the Son of God." This suggests that when Philip "preached Jesus," he preached that he was God's Son.

The second title affirming Jesus' divine nature may surprise some. It is the title, "Son of Man." A common idea is that this refers to Jesus' human nature, but this was not the connotation attached to it in first-century religious circles. It was instead a very exalted title, one that signified a status of supernatural glory. The apocryphal book of Enoch applies it to a supernatural, heavenly figure who judges men and angels on the day of judgment. Daniel 7:13, 14 depicts the Son of Man as a heavenly figure appearing before the "Ancient of Days" to receive an eternal kingdom and universal worship.

It was Jesus' favorite title for himself during his earthly ministry. As Son of Man, he ascribed glory and power to himself:

"The Son of Man is Lord of the Sabbath" (Matthew 12:8). "The Son of Man has authority on earth to forgive sins," a prerogative belonging to God alone (Mark 2:7, 10). The Son of Man will come in the clouds in the glory of his Father with great power and with the angels (Mark 8:38; 13:26), and will sit on his glorious throne and judge the nations (Matthew 16:27; 25:31, 32).

Bible students agree that "Son of Man" is an exalted declaration of majesty, even the "greatest and most celestial of all titles."

The third main title of deity is "Lord" *(Kurios* in Greek). In New Testament times this word had several levels of meaning. It was a term of respectful address (equivalent to "sir," as in "Yes, sir") and a title of honor (equivalent to "lord," as in "Lord Henry Brenthrop"). Its generic meaning is "owner," as in "landlord." When we confess Jesus as our Lord, we are acknowledging (for one thing) that he is our owner.

Also, *kurios* was used as a title for those thought to be divine. It was applied to pagan deities, including the Roman Caesars who claimed to be gods. Under Roman persecution Christians were given the choice of proclaiming Caesar as lord *(kurios),* or Jesus as Lord. (See 1 Corinthians 12:2, 3.)

Most significant, however, is the way this term was used in the Greek translation of the Old Testament, the Septuagint, which was widely used by Jews in the first century. In most manuscripts, *kurios* is the term used to translate or represent the most sacred Hebrew name of God, Yahweh (YHWH) or Jehovah. More than six thousand times God is called *Kurios,* almost one thousand times in the expression "Lord God" *(Kurios ho Theos).*

Why is this significant? Because any Jew who knew his Greek Old Testament would have associated this title immediately with the one true God. This is certainly the case with the apostle Paul and other New Testament writers, who frequently used the wording of the Septuagint version when quoting the Old Testament.

It is significant, then, that the New Testament writers used this title frequently—with Paul, almost exclusively—*for Jesus!* There is no way they could have applied this title to Jesus in its religious sense without in their minds identifying him with Yahweh himself, thus equating him with God.

Even before he was born, Jesus was confessed as Lord. Under inspiration, Elizabeth called her cousin Mary "the mother of my Lord" (Luke 1:41-43). (This is especially significant in view of the way "Lord" is used of God the Father throughout Luke 1.) Thomas addressed the risen Christ as "my Lord and my God"

(John 20:28). When early Christians confessed Jesus as Lord (Romans 10:9; 1 Corinthians 12:3), they were confessing his deity.

Jesus is the Son of God; Jesus is the Son of Man; Jesus is Lord. The common nuance shared by all three of these titles is simply this: Jesus is God.

Jesus Is Identified as God

In addition to these titles, there are many biblical passages that specifically call Jesus God. Perhaps most striking are those texts that identify Jesus with Yahweh of the Old Testament. We have already seen how the title "Lord" *(Kurios)* points in this direction. In addition to this, several Old Testament statements or prophecies specifically about Yahweh are quoted in the New Testament as referring to Jesus. For example, Matthew 3:3 says that Isaiah 40:3 refers to John the Baptist's ministry as the forerunner of the Messiah: "Make ready the way of the Lord, make His paths straight!" But Isaiah 40:3 speaks unequivocally of Yahweh: "Clear the way for the Lord [Yahweh] in the wilderness; make smooth in the desert a highway for our God."

Also, Psalm 102:25-27 (which refers to Yahweh; see v. 12) is cited of Jesus in Hebrews 1:10-12; Deuteronomy 10:17 is cited of him in Revelation 17:14 and 19:16; and Isaiah 45:23 is cited of him in Philippians 2:10, 11. Especially important is Joel 2:32, "And it will come about that whoever calls on the name of the Lord [Yahweh] will be delivered." Twice the New Testament quotes this verse and refers it to Jesus (Acts 2:21 [see v. 36] and Romans 10:9, 13).

This identification of Jesus with Yahweh does not mean that Jesus *alone* is Yahweh, but that Yahweh *includes* Jesus. Or, strictly speaking, Yahweh includes the eternal *Logos* (John 1:1) who became incarnate upon this earth as Jesus of Nazareth. In other words, Yahweh, the Lord God of the Old Testament, is now known to be a trinity of Father, Son, and Holy Spirit (Matthew 28:19). The Son of God is literally God the Son.

Numerous other Bible passages speak of Jesus as God. The grand nativity prophecy in Isaiah 9:6 calls him "Mighty God." Psalm 45:6 says, "Thy throne, O God, is forever and ever'" and Hebrews 1:8, 9 says this refers to Jesus. John 1:1 says, "In the beginning was the Word, and the Word was with God, and *the Word was God*" (my emphasis). Verse 14 says this divine Word became flesh as Jesus. Thomas confessed the risen Christ as "my Lord and my God" (John 20:28). Acts 20:28 refers to "the church of God which He purchased with His own blood."

Philippians 2:6 says that Jesus, when he preexisted as the *Logos*, was existing in the very form of God; and his equality with God was not something he had to grasp after—because he already had it! It is very important not to misinterpret Philippians 2:7 (Jesus "emptied Himself") as saying that he laid aside his deity or emptied himself of his divine nature. This is absolutely untrue. It means only that he laid aside his privileges or prerogatives as God. Even in him as a human being, "all the fulness of Deity dwells in bodily form" (Colossians 2:9).

Jesus Is Worshiped as God

A final indication of the deity of Jesus is that he was and is worshiped by creatures, accepting it without rebuke. This is significant since worship of any creature rather than the Creator is severely condemned in Romans 1:25. Holy creatures always refuse worship and direct it toward God (Acts 10:25, 26; 14:11-15; Revelation 19:10; 22:8, 9). When Satan tempted Jesus to worship him, Jesus replied, "You shall worship the Lord your God, and serve Him only" (Matthew 4:9, 10).

Yet Jesus himself accepted worship from the healed blind man (John 9:38) and from Thomas (John 20:28). Moreover, he declared that it is the Father's will "that all may honor the Son, even as they honor the Father" (John 5:23). The term "even as" *(kathos* in Greek) indicates that the Son is to receive equal honor with the Father.

The angels worshiped Jesus at his birth (Luke 2:13, 14) in obedience to the Father's command: "Let all the angels of God worship Him" (Hebrew 1:6). They continue to worship him even now as he sits at the right hand of the Father (Revelation 5:8-14). "Every created thing" gives equal honor "to Him who sits on the throne, and to the Lamb" (v. 13).

The Virgin Birth of Jesus

That the Bible teaches the divine nature of Christ can scarcely be disputed. A teaching closely associated with his deity is the doctrine of his virgin birth. The title of a book by Robert

Gromacki correctly reflects this connection: *The Virgin Birth: Doctrine of Deity.* Gromacki says,

> If the Biblical presentation of the person of Jesus Christ is correct, then He must have been God. Once this is accepted, it is only logical to assert that His entrance into the world must have been supernatural. There was only one means that could properly provide the channel for His incarnation: THE VIRGIN BIRTH.[1]

Thus "to confess the virgin birth is to confess the deity of Christ; to confess the deity of Christ is to confess the virgin birth."[2]

Other births recorded in the Bible were supernaturally caused in the sense that one or both parents were barren or beyond the age of natural childbearing. This includes Isaac (Genesis 18:9-14), Samuel (1 Samuel 1:1-20), and John the Baptist (Luke 1:5-25). But these births were all different from the birth of Jesus in that they involved two human parents and produced ordinary human children. The virgin birth of Jesus was unique in that it involved only one human parent and produced an offspring who was both fully human and fully divine.

The virgin birth of Jesus was foretold in Isaiah 7:14: "Behold, a virgin will be with child and bear a son, and she will call His name Immanuel." Matthew records the virgin birth of Jesus from Joseph's perspective, declaring that it is the fulfillment of Isaiah 7:14 (Matthew 1:18-25). Luke records it from Mary's perspective (Luke 1:26-35). Paul does not specifically mention the virgin birth, but whenever he refers to the birth of Jesus (Romans 1:3; Galatians 4:4; Philippians 2:7), he uses the Greek word *ginomai* ("become, come into being") and avoids the word *gennao*, the common term for "be born" which has the connotation of paternal begetting.

Explanation of the Virgin Birth

The virgin birth is a unique event that will always be shrouded in mystery. While we cannot explain the mechanics of this miracle, we can understand some general facets of it in light of biblical teaching.

First, it was not a natural event and has no resemblance to any kind of natural birth, human or animal. In some lower species of animals, unfertilized female eggs normally develop into males or females of the species. This is called "parthenogenesis": virgin birth. Through artificial stimulation eggs from some other species, including mammalian, have been induced to develop into normal animals. In mammals, however, because of chromosomal distribution, the offspring are always female. There simply are no natural parallels to and no natural explanations for the virgin birth of Christ.

Second, the conception of Jesus was not the result of a corporal sexual coupling between Mary and Deity with a body. Greek mythology sometimes portrays Olympian deities mating with human beings in this fashion. Mormon theology, which portrays God as having a humanlike body, explains Jesus' conception in this way.[3] Contrary to all such notions, the virgin birth of Jesus was not a sexual event in any sense in reference to its cause.

Third, the virgin birth was not just the *ex nihilo* creation of the person Jesus, who was simply housed within and nourished by Mary's womb. The human nature of Jesus began as an ovum produced by Mary. He was literally Mary's offspring or "seed." Otherwise he would not really be a part of the human race and would not be physically descended from Eve (Genesis 3:15), from Abraham (Genesis 22:18; Galatians 3:16), and from David (2 Samuel 7:12; Romans 1:3).

Fourth, the supernatural act of God that brought Jesus into the world was not at his birth as such but at his conception. So we could more precisely speak of his "virgin conception." This was the point of time when the new and specific person known as Jesus first came into being and Mary's ovum began to grow.

This is comparable to the beginning of other human persons. Each of us began our new existence as the result of the union of two preexisting entities: our father's sperm and our mother's ovum. But in the case of Jesus there was no paternal sperm. The two preexisting entities that came together to initiate his existence were Mary's ovum and the eternal, personal, divine Word *(Logos)*, God the Son (John 1:1-3). At the appointed time the pre-existing *Logos* entered into some unexplainable union with the ovum. At this point, through the power of the Holy Spirit (Matthew 1:20; Luke 1:35), a new and unique individual came into existence, as the divine person of the *Logos* was incorporated into the fully human personhood of the nanoseconds-old Jesus.

Fifth, the result of this virgin conception was indeed unique. Jesus was the incarnation (enfleshment) of God in a human person. "The Word became flesh, and dwelt among us" (John 1:14;

see Hebrews 2:14). This does not mean that the divine *Logos* simply occupied a human body; rather, he was united with a whole human person. Jesus had a human body *and* a human spirit. Also, this does not mean that God was *transformed into* a human person. The incarnation was rather a joining of God and man in a way that preserved the integrity of both natures, a way that is not understandable by us.

Sixth, from the point of conception onward, the unique person Jesus continued to develop in Mary's womb in a natural way until the time of birth, under the protection of the Father. The birth itself occurred in a natural way, except, of course, that Mary was still a virgin when the birth occurred.

Seventh, it is obvious that Jesus had only one earthly parent: his mother, Mary. Joseph was his father only in a legal sense (see Luke 2:27, 41; 4:22) and was his official guardian. Matthew's genealogy of Jesus (1:1-17) is probably that of Joseph, while Luke's (3:23-38) is probably Mary's.[4]

Significance of the Virgin Birth

What is the rationale for the virgin birth of Christ? Why did the Savior come into the world in this fashion? Why was it necessary?

It should be obvious that the doctrine of the virgin birth is not a doctrine about Mary, but about Jesus. Mary's submissive obedience is highly commendable and her privilege unmatched, but she is not the focal point of this event.

It should be stressed, too, that the virgin birth was not essential as a mechanism for preserving Jesus from "original sin," though many have tried to give it this significance. As James Taylor wrote in a *Christianity Today* article, because of his miraculous conception, "this Child of Mary's womb does not stand in the fallen sequence of Adam, sharing mankind's guilt and sin," or "man's foul taint."[5]

There is no basis for this idea, however. Some would reject it because they see no biblical evidence of a concept of original sin in the first place. But even if there is some sort of inherited "taint," God could have miraculously preserved Jesus from it without the necessity of a virgin conception.

The only real significance of the virgin birth lies in its necessary relation to the deity of Jesus. To perform the great saving works of atonement and resurrection, the Redeemer must be a sinless human being who is also God. The virgin birth is the means by which such a person has come into being.

The virgin birth is a means, not an end. Its main point is not the birth itself, but the divine nature of the one born thereby. As the angel announced to Mary, "The holy offspring shall be called the Son of God" (Luke 1:35). Because he is virgin-born through the power of the Holy Spirit, his name is Immanuel, "God with us" (Isaiah 7:14; Matthew 1:23). The virgin birth is thus the means by which the divine Savior was born, and it is the guarantee to us of his deity.

The result of the virgin birth is that Jesus is one person with two natures. He is not a unique kind of schizophrenic with a divine person living inside his body along with his human personality. As one person, he has just one mind, one center of consciousness. He has both a fully human nature, with a human body and human spirit, and a fully divine nature.

Such a unique person requires a unique birth. This is why the early fundamentalists included the virgin birth in their list of fundamentals. Liberals were denying not just the virgin birth, but the true deity of Christ as well. In their view, the "divinity" of Jesus was simply his ethical oneness with the Father's will. His "divine" nature was not qualitatively different from ours. We have the potential to be just as "divine" as Jesus was, they asserted.

The fundamentalists rightly called this heresy and defended the true deity of Christ, with acceptance of the virgin birth being the touchstone for this doctrine.

Why Is the Deity of Jesus Essential?

Let's return the focus to the deity of Jesus. That Jesus is God is indeed an essential doctrine of Christianity. It is not just an arbitrary fact presented to us to test our faith. It is absolutely necessary for the whole work of redemption.

Periodically we find those among us who suggest that one may have a true saving faith in Jesus without accepting him as being equal with God. As long as someone believes Jesus is the Messiah, they say, why should anything more be required? Do we really have to agree with the Nicene Creed, that Jesus is of the same essence or substance as the Father?

The answer is yes, for two reasons. First, Jesus' equality with God is not just a fourth-century interpretation of the New Testament; it is the specific teaching of the Bible itself. Second, one cannot accept Jesus as the Messiah without also accepting his divine nature. This is seen in Peter's inspired confession that Jesus is both the *Christ* and the *Son of God* (Matthew 16:16).

Jesus' saviorhood and deity are inseparable. His deity is essential to his being able to do what the New Testament says he has done, both in his atonement and in his resurrection.

Deity and Atonement

As we saw in the last chapter, the essence of the atonement is that Jesus gave himself as a substitute to suffer the penalty for sin in our place. Some challenge this idea on the grounds that it is immoral to punish an innocent person in the place of the guilty one who actually deserves it, even if the former is willing.

This could be true if the innocent substitute were just an indifferent third party picked at random to suffer the divine Lawgiver's wrath on behalf of the guilty lawbreaker. But this is not the case. Because the Substitute is himself the divine *Logos* in human form, he is not just an innocent bystander in the matter. He is the eternal lawgiver and judge himself, suffering the penalty of his own law.

The point is, as H. E. Guillebaud says, that substitutionary atonement "is not defensible apart from a full recognition of the Bible teaching of the Divinity of Christ. For if the Victim is not truly identical with the Judge, then the sacrifice is of a third party, and becomes unjust."[6] Thus Christ's deity is a prerequisite of the saving efficacy of the cross.

Another challenge to the substitutionary atonement is that it is logically impossible for just one person to pay the penalty for all the sins of the whole world. Since the penalty involves physical and eternal death, and since any one person has only *one* life to give, *one* individual could be a substitute for only one other.

We grant this to be true, *if* the substitute is only an ordinary human being not qualitatively different from those whose penalty he is bearing. One finite person could not possibly pay the penalty for more that one other finite person.

But here is the essentiality of the divine nature of Jesus. He is not just a finite creature. In his divine nature he is the infinite God. When he suffered for our sins, he suffered not just in his physical human body but in his divine nature as well. Such suffering was *infinite* and thus sufficient for all the sins of the whole world. The infinite nature of the divine Savior's suffering was more than equivalent to the eternal punishment in hell for every member of the human race.

One other requirement for the atonement was that the substitute had to be sinless. If Jesus had committed even one sin, he himself would have deserved to die and thus would not have qualified as a substitute for us. But he was sinless (2 Corinthians 5:21; Hebrews 4:15) and so was an acceptable substitute. The only way this sinlessness could be guaranteed from the beginning is if he were divine. Since Jesus was God, he could not sin. (Though not everyone agrees with this point, I affirm it without hesitation.)

Deity and Resurrection

Others besides Jesus have been raised from the dead. By God's miraculous power any dead person can be renewed to physical life. Jesus did not have to be divine to experience resurrection. But his resurrection was much more than this. When he arose from the dead, Jesus was not merely the *recipient* of God's life-giving power, he was its very *source*. The resurrection of Jesus was the unleashing of universal, infinite power.

This power defeated our enemy, death, and the one who wielded it against us like a sword, namely, Satan. No mere man could have won this victory, and even Michael the archangel had to call on God to overcome Satan's opposition (Jude 9). But Jesus is more than a man and more than an angel. He is God enfleshed, the embodiment of all power and authority (Matthew 28:18). Thus his victory over Satan and death was never in doubt.

The infinite power that flows from the risen Christ is able to redeem the universe itself, including our own mortal bodies (Romans 8:18-23). This is not merely a restoration of the old, original order of things, but an advance to a new and eternal and glorified state. Such an act of redemption is a combination of resurrection and creation—the two masterworks in the repertoire of divine omnipotence (Romans 4:17). It is the work of deity, the work of God's Son, Jesus.

Gromacki was correct when he wrote, "Only if Jesus was God could He rightfully be called the object of saving faith."[6] Without his deity, and without his virgin birth as the sure vehicle thereof, there is no gospel of salvation and no such thing as Christianity in its original and true sense.

[1] Robert Glenn Gromacki, *The Virgin Birth: Doctrine of Deity* (Nelson, 1974), 68.

[2] Ibid., 189.

[3] For shocking quotations on this point see Jerald and Sandra Tanner, *The Changing World of Mormonism* (Moody, 1980), 179–182.

[4] See Gromacki, ch. 17.

[5] James Taylor, "Born of a Virgin," *Christianity Today*, December 18, 1964: 282.

[6] H. E. Guillebaud, *Why the Cross,* 2 ed. (London: InterVarsity Fellowship, 1946), 148.

[7] Gromacki, 31.

Fundamental #6

We Are Saved by Grace, Through Faith, in Baptism

Imagine a great Kingdom ruled by a kind and benevolent King. In this Kingdom of Love and Light the citizens are happy and content and protected by the Great King, who supplies them with everything they truly need. In return they are required only to rely on the Great King and try to obey his laws.

Everyone knows, though, that the Enemy Kingdom across the sea claims to be much better. Rumors of great pleasure, untold prosperity, and unlimited freedom abound. Its agents constantly lure the servants of the Great King to defect and to join them across the sea, offering convenient transportation on clandestine smuggling ships.

Many are seduced by this offer and leave the good Kingdom for the rival shores. They arrive euphoric with expectation, and at first everything seems wonderful. But before long many begin to notice a sinister hollowness in the way of life in the Enemy Kingdom. They are not as happy as they thought they would be.

Then they discover the truth: it is all a hoax. The real situation is gruesome and fearsome. The Enemy King is a cruel tyrant, and everyone is actually his slave. The bland food and polluted water are dangerously low; drought and famine threaten. Many are dying of starvation and disease and violence. Crime and anarchy are all around.

But there is good news! The Great King knows the plight of those who have defected to the Enemy Kingdom. And even though they have rejected him and rebelled against him, he wants them back. At great expense he has constructed a fleet of rescue ships that offer a free return shuttle back to the Kingdom of Love and Light. There is always one anchored offshore at the Enemy Kingdom, waiting.

A loudspeaker pleads for anyone and everyone to come back to the Great King, who offers a complete pardon and complete rehabilitation in his Kingdom. The loudspeaker broadcasts the clear and simple instructions on how to escape the cruel tyrant and how to get on the rescue ship.

The main elements of this allegory should be clear. The Great King is God. The Enemy King is Satan. Those who allow themselves to be seduced by the Enemy King are sinners. The fleet of rescue ships represent the redemption accomplished through Jesus.

This chapter focuses on the last part of the allegory: the instructions on how to escape the tyrant and get on the ship. This represents the biblical instruction on how to be saved.

The gospel of Jesus Christ must include not only an explanation of Christ's work and the salvation brought about by that work; it must also include instruction on how sinners may access this salvation. Without such instruction, the work of Christ would be in vain.

As an illustration, I have a friend with heart trouble who once told me he was taking *ten* kinds of medicine. I picture his physician telling him he can be cured if he just takes the right pills. The physician then gives him ten prescriptions. My friend takes them to a pharmacist, who takes ten large bottles of pills from his shelf and dumps about fifty of each into a large paper bag. He shakes them up and hands the bag to my friend, with no instructions as to how many of which pills to take how often! But without such instructions, my sick friend may as well have no medicine at all.

The fact is that the basic instruction on how to be saved is one of the essentials of the Christian faith. Unfortunately, this point was not included in the early twentieth-century list of fundamentals. It is abundantly set forth, however, in the earliest gospel preaching recorded in the book of Acts and in the New Testament as a whole. When we examine this data we find that a sinner is saved *by grace, through faith, in baptism.*

Saved by Grace

The gospel is the good news about how salvation is accomplished by Jesus Christ and him alone: "And there is salvation in no one else; for there is no other name under heaven that has been given among men, by which we must saved" (Acts 4:12).

The gospel is also the good news about how this salvation can be received by sinners. In the most general sense, one accepts God's offer by *turning to the Lord* (Acts 9:35), which includes *repenting* (Acts 3:19) and *calling on his name* (Acts 2:21; Romans 10:13). Specific instructions are given as to how one does this in Acts 2:38; 16:30-33; 22:16; and elsewhere in the New Testament.

The God of Grace

The most amazing thing about salvation is why God would even do it in the first place, especially since it can be accomplished only by such an extreme solution as the incarnation and atonement. In terms of the allegory, why would the Great King even *want* to rescue the rebels, much less go to the great expense of building a fleet of rescue ships? Why would he not just say, "Good riddance!" Or why would he not just launch a few ICBMs and wipe out the Enemy Kingdom, tyrant and slaves alike?

The fact that God even wants to save us and has actually done everything to make it possible shows there is something about his nature that is far different from the usual pagan concept of God.

It is typical of non-Christians and unbelievers of all kinds to think of God (if at all) in one of two ways. On the one hand, God is pictured as stern and strict, severe and austere, unyielding and demanding. He is full of negatives and imperatives, wrath and justice. On the other hand, God is seen as kind, easygoing, softhearted, loving, doting, generous, lenient, sympathetic, forgiving, and blind to our faults.

Is this wrong? Does not the Bible portray God as stern, severe, and wrathful? Yes! And does it not picture him as kind and loving and generous? Yes! So what is the problem? Just this: in pagan eyes God's character conforms to either one or the other of these two descriptions, but not to both. They seem to be contradictory or incompatible.

However problematic this may seem, the Bible makes it clear that both of these descriptions apply to the true God at the same time! God is simultaneously a holy and just lawgiver, and a good and loving giftgiver. This presents no problem at all in a pure universe. But once sin enters through the freewill choices of created beings, these two sides of God's nature come into real tension. When confronted by sin, God's holy nature breaks forth in *wrath*, a "consuming fire" that must devour his enemies (Hebrews 12:29). At the same time his loving nature expresses itself as *grace*, which desires to save his enemies (John 3:16).

How does God resolve this tension and remain true to both his wrath and his grace at the same time? Only through the atoning sacrifice of the cross. By pouring out his wrath upon God the Son as a substitute, the Father both satisfies his righteous wrath and makes it possible to save the sinner in spite of his sins (Romans 3:26). The side of the cross that faces God absorbs his wrath; the side that faces us pours forth his grace.

The good news is not that God has no wrath, but that the God of wrath is also a God of grace.

The Call of Grace

This is the amazing thing about grace: Though we have sinned, God wants us back! He seeks us, pleads with us, begs us with outstretched arms to return to him. "I permitted Myself to be sought by those who did not ask for Me; I permitted Myself to be found by those who did not seek Me. I said, 'Here am I, here am I,' to a nation which did not call on My name. I have spread out My hands all day long to a rebellious people" (Isaiah 65:1, 2). "O Jerusalem, Jerusalem," cried Jesus to his people, "how often I wanted to gather your children together, the way a hen gathers her chicks under her wings, and you were unwilling" (Matthew 23:37).

This is the deepest stratum of the heart of God. The crossbar of Jesus' cross is well likened to God's ever-outspread arms, asking the sinner to come home.

The gospel call, the call of grace, is God's simple plea: "Turn! Turn away from sin, and return to me." This way of speaking appears often in Acts. Many "turned to the Lord" (9:35). "A large number who believed turned to the Lord" (11:21). The Gentiles are exhorted to "turn from these vain things to a living God" (14:15). The church rejoiced that many Gentiles were "turning to God" (15:19). Saul (Paul) was commissioned to preach to the Gentiles "that they may turn from darkness to light and from the dominion of Satan to God" (26:18; see 26:20). Also see 28:27.

The general act of turning has two aspects. It is first of all a turning *away* from vain idols, from the darkness of willful ignorance and sin, and from the Enemy King (Acts 14:15; 26:18). The name for this "turning away" is *repentance.* "Repent therefore and return," said Peter to the Jews (Acts 3:19). "Repent and turn to God," said Paul to both Jews and Gentiles (Acts 26:20). The gospel call was a call to repent (Acts 2:38; 17:30; 20:21).

Repentance is not just a subpoint or aspect of faith. It is the sinner's admission of the awfulness of his rebellion against the Great King and of the heinousness of his sins. It comes when the sinner opens his eyes to the seriousness of sin and begins to abhor and hate his own sin. It is a "River Kwai" experience, such as occurred when the British officer in the prisoner-of-war camp realized what he had done in pressing his men to build the railroad bridge that would carry destruction to his own allies. "What have I done?" is the cry of repentance.

Grace calls the sinner not only to turn *away* from sin but also to turn *toward* God and his Kingdom of Love and Light (Acts 14:15; 26:18). The name for this "turning toward" is *calling on the name of the Lord* (Acts 2:21; 22:16; Romans 10:9-17). Hearing the call of grace, the sinner turns and calls upon the gracious God to receive him and bestow the promised salvation.

The call of grace is not to be regarded as a legalistic demand, but as a gracious opportunity. God is not just *demanding* that we turn to him; he is *inviting* us to do so. Many sinners are afraid to turn toward God. They are afraid they will see a fierce and fearsome face of wrath and brimstone. But if we turn while God is calling, we will see the tender face of the Father and the outstretched arms of Jesus on the cross, welcoming us back.

Scripture speaks of repentance as something God grants both to Israel and the Gentiles (Acts 5:31; 11:18). That is, he grants them the *opportunity* to repent and turn to him. The call to "repent and turn" comes not from the Lawgiver laying more law on the already overburdened sinner; it comes as part of the gospel (Acts 14:15). It is part of the good news that is announced (Acts 17:30; 26:20). The word used is *apangello,* which can be used for telling good news, as in Matthew 12:18. (See the parallel in Luke 4:18, 19.)

The Content of Grace

When called to turn away from sin and turn toward God, what will sinners receive if they respond? What is on that rescue ship they are invited to board? The content of grace may be described as a *double cure.*

The first aspect of the double cure is the cancellation of sin's guilt and penalty. This act is called justification—we are "justified as a gift by His grace through the redemption which is in Christ Jesus" (Romans 3:24).

Justification is the act of a judge in a courtroom when he declares the defendant to be free from all penalty. We as sinners are justified when God as judge looks us in the eye and says, "No penalty for you!" How can this be, since we deserve the penalty? It is possible only because Jesus has already paid the penalty for all sin. When we turn to God, the suffering of Jesus is imputed to us, or entered into our account, thus canceling all the penalty-debt we owe to God. This state of being debt-free is complete from the moment we first receive the gift of justification.

Other biblical expressions equivalent to justification are forgiveness of sins (Acts 2:38; 10:43; 13:38; 26:18), the wiping away of sins (Acts 3:19), and the washing away of sins (Acts 22:16).

The second aspect of the double cure of grace is setting the sinner free from his sin-sickness and spiritual bondage to sin. This is a lifelong process that begins with an act called regeneration and continues in ongoing sanctification or "growing in grace and knowledge." Through this process the sinner is not just *declared* righteous (as in justification) but is actually *made* righteous. This is accomplished by the power of the indwelling Holy Spirit, whom is given to every sinner who turns to God.

From the very beginning, the "gift of the Holy Spirit" has been part of the content of grace (Acts 2:38). With this gift come "times of refreshing" (Acts 3:19) and being "freed from all things" (Acts 13:39). The life-giving Spirit is the main element of the "inheritance among those who have been sanctified by faith in Me" (Acts 26:18; see Galatians 3:1–4:7).

Saved Through Faith

What leads a sinner to turn to the Lord, that is, to repent and call on his name? The answer is *faith.* The sinner turns when he finally believes what the Bible says about his position before the law of God and what the Bible says about the way of salvation. Faith is born when the sinner says, "It's true. Here in the Enemy

Kingdom I'm a dying slave. If I stay here, I'm lost. It's also true that the Great King really loves me and wants me back. I believe what the loudspeaker is saying, that there's a boat waiting to take me back to the Kingdom of Love and Light. I'm ready to go back!" In this way people who *believe* turn to the Lord (Acts 11:21).

Faith in God's Word—both his law and his gospel—is thus a necessary means of receiving the content of saving grace. This is acknowledged by practically all Bible believers. And since it is necessary to have faith in order to be saved, the doctrine of the essentiality of faith must itself be an essential doctrine. It is part of the bull's-eye.

The necessity of faith is implicit in every presentation of the gospel recorded in Acts, and explicit in many contexts. Paul declares that "everyone who believes is freed from all things" (13:39; see 14:23). The Philippian jailer was told to "believe in the Lord Jesus" to be saved (16:31; see 16:34). Crispus, his household, and many other Corinthians "believed in the Lord" (18:8). Paul's gospel included "repentance toward God and faith in our Lord Jesus Christ" (20:21). We can be sanctified only "by faith" in the Lord (26:18).

Though the text of Acts 8:37 is questioned by many, it accurately reflects the belief and practice of the early church and the teaching of the New Testament. While Philip was preaching, the eunuch asked to be baptized. Philip's reply, according to verse 37, was, "If you believe with all your heart, you may." Believe *what?* someone may ask. Since Philip was preaching about Jesus, we must assume he was talking about faith in Jesus. The eunuch's reply makes this clear: "I believe that Jesus Christ is the Son of God."

Exactly what is faith? Some divide it into three parts, some into four or more. Probably two are sufficient. Faith is first of all *assenting* to the truth of certain statements, such as the "essentials": believing *that* God exists (Hebrew 11:6), believing *that* Jesus rose from the dead (Romans 10:9), and the rest. Such faith is an act of the intellect responding to the adequacy of evidence.

Faith is also *trusting* a person enough to take him at his word and to rely on him. Such faith is directed toward Jesus. It is a decision of the will to place yourself and all that is dear to you in his hands, a decision to trust your eternity to the sufficiency of his death and resurrection (2 Timothy 1:12). In biblical terminology it is believing *in* or believing *on* Jesus (John 3:16; Acts 16:31).

In terms of our allegory, faith is first of all believing that the message broadcast over the ship's loudspeaker is true—that the Great King still loves you and wants you back, that a boat is really waiting for you, and that you will not be punished if you turn to him now. But just believing that all this is true is not enough. Faith must also include the personal decision to act on the accepted truth—to forsake the Enemy King, place your future in the hands of the Great King, and board his rescue ship. Just believing, without a personal decision to act on that belief, is vain.

The fact that faith is the means of receiving salvation is not just an arbitrary condition chosen by God. Given the nature of salvation, it is a *necessary* condition. This is because the actual source of our salvation lies in something that has been done by someone else—Jesus. We can be saved only by accepting and relying on what he has done as being sufficient for us. This act of relying on him (instead of ourselves) is the very essence of faith.

The slaves who are slowing dying in the Enemy Kingdom can be saved only by escaping that kingdom altogether. But they cannot save themselves by their own works. They cannot swim the distance, and there is nothing with which to build a boat or raft. The only hope is the rescue ship of the Great King. The choices are simple: accept his offer and get in the ship, or die miserably.

This is why the Bible says we are saved by grace through faith, and not as the result of our own works (Ephesians 2:8, 9). We are saved *for* good works (Ephesians 2:10). That is, the rescue ship carries us back to the Kingdom of Love and Light where we are enabled by the indwelling Spirit to live a God-fearing and fruitful life. But the only way to get back to this Kingdom is to accept the results of the King's work on our behalf.

Saved in Baptism

What is Christian baptism? It is *immersion*. Something is baptized when it is dipped or immersed into water or some other liquid. The Greek word was used for dipping a garment into a pot of dye or for the sinking of a ship into the sea. It was used figuratively for being overwhelmed by feelings such as fear or desire.

Thus biblical baptism is immersion, not sprinkling or dabbing or pouring. John chose a specific locale for his baptizing ministry "because there was much water there" (John 3:23). When Philip baptized the eunuch, "they both went down into the water" (Acts 8:38), an action totally unnecessary for anything except immersion.

What is Christian baptism? It is immersion *in water.* The New Testament says that Christians are immersed in the Holy Spirit (1 Corinthians 12:13), but in normal circumstances this is never separated from being immersed in water. Thus there is just "one baptism" (Ephesians 4:5), with the Holy Spirit overwhelming our spirit even as the water receives our body. The "baptism of the Spirit" on Pentecost (Acts 2) and for Cornelius (Acts 10) was miraculously separated from baptism in water for evidential purposes.

In response to Philip's preaching, the eunuch cried out, "Look! Water! What prevents me from being baptized?" (Acts 8:36). This shows that when Philip told the eunuch about baptism they both understood it to be baptism in water. "Our bodies," says Hebrews 10:22, have been "washed with pure water," unlike certain Old Testament cleansing ceremonies that required a mixture of animal blood and water.

What is Christian baptism? It is the immersion of *a believer* in water. A person not old enough to consciously turn to God in repentance and faith does not *need* baptism and receives no benefit from being immersed into water. Immersion is for those old enough to understand their condition as guilty sinners under the condemnation of the law, and old enough to understand and accept the gospel message of salvation through Jesus Christ.

Scripture consistently presents baptism as being preceded by the conscious acts of repentance and faith. "He who has believed and has been baptized shall be saved" (Mark 16:16). "Repent, and let each of you be baptized" (Acts 2:38). "And many of the Corinthians when they heard were believing and being baptized" (Acts 18:8). In Samaria when men and women believed, they were baptized (Acts 8:12). According to Acts 8:37, Philip told the eunuch he could be baptized *if* he believed.

Some assume that when a "household" was baptized (Acts 16:33), this must have included infants and small children. This is unfounded speculation, however. In the case of the Philippian jailer, Paul specifically stated that believing in Jesus was the primary prerequisite for salvation (Acts 16:31). Paul then "spoke the word of the Lord to him together with all who were in his house" (16:32). Everyone who was in his "household" was thus old enough to hear and understand the Word of God. Verse 34 says specifically that "his whole household" believed.

What is Christian baptism? It is part of the apostolic presentation of *the gospel.* When the Jews at Pentecost asked how to be free from their sins, Peter told them to repent and be baptized (Acts 2:38). The Samaritans who believed were baptized (Acts 8:12, 13). One of the first things God's messenger Ananias said to the starving, blind, contrite Saul of Tarsus was "Arise, and be baptized, and wash away your sins" (Acts 22:16; see 9:18). When Cornelius and his household received the miraculous outpouring of the Spirit, the first thing Peter told them to do was be baptized (Acts 10:47, 48). Paul's message to Lydia (Acts 16:14, 15), to the Philippian jailer (Acts 16:30-33), and to the Corinthians (Acts 18:8) included baptism. In his instruction to the Ephesian disciples (Acts 19:1-5), Paul makes it clear that the full gospel includes Christian baptism and that faith itself is ineffective without it. (Compare verse 2 and verse 5.)

This could hardly be any clearer than it is in the account of Philip and the eunuch in Acts 8. As Philip was preaching the gospel, the eunuch's very first response was "Look! Water! What prevents me from being baptized?" (8:36). But how can this be? Philip was preaching *Jesus* to the man (8:35). What does his response have to do with Jesus?

This whole episode shows that when Philip preached the gospel, he spoke not only of what Jesus did to save us, but also of what the sinner must do to receive that salvation. The goal of his preaching was not just to bring the eunuch to faith, but also to baptize him into Christ. Baptism was part of his gospel message.

We must remember that Philip was teaching a non-Christian, not instructing a Christian on how to live an obedient life. Baptism is part of the former, not the latter. The eunuch's query about baptism was the response of a non-Christian seeking to become a Christian. After he had been baptized, and not before, he "went on his way rejoicing" (8:39).

The only reasonable conclusion to draw from all of this—and this is the clear teaching of the whole New Testament—is that baptism is part of the *turning* process, just as faith is part of it. Faith is the state of the heart that causes us to turn to God for salvation; baptism is the point of time when God actually bestows the double cure of grace. It is a saving event, the place where the sinner meets Jesus and receives salvation.

In our allegory, the rescue ship is anchored a bit offshore. When the stranded rebel makes his move to enter the boat, he must go into the water in order to reach it. As he goes down into the water, he steps off the shore of the Enemy Kingdom. When he comes up out of the water, he is in the ship of redemption.

Every New Testament text that deals with the meaning of baptism makes it the point of salvation.[1] He that believes and is baptized shall be saved (Mark 16:16). Baptism does also now save us (1 Peter 3:21). We are baptized into Christ, into his death and resurrection (Romans 6:3, 4; Galatians 3:27; Colossians 2:12). Baptism is the washing away of sins (Acts 22:16). Baptism is for the remission of sins and the gift of the Holy Spirit: the double cure (Acts 2:38). In baptism we are buried with Christ and raised up with him: the double cure (Colossians 2:12). It is the time of the new birth (John 3:3-5). It is the washing that brings regeneration and renewing through the Holy Spirit (Titus 3:5). It brings us into the body of Christ, the invisible church (1 Corinthians 12:13).

Those who think such a view of baptism is contrary to salvation by grace have made the error of identifying baptism as a human work. This is not biblical. Jesus himself separated baptism from the category of commandments to be obeyed as a part of Christian growth (Matthew 28:19, 20). Everything that baptism is depicted as accomplishing is a work of God, not a work of man. We must agree with Martin Luther: baptism is a work, but it is *God's* work, not man's. This is the essence of grace.

The Whole Gospel

The gospel instruction on how to be saved is a "fundamental," an aspect of essential doctrine. This aspect of the gospel says to the sinner first of all that, even though you have sinned, God loves you and wants you back. He will wipe away all that you owe him and wipe away all your tears. He will receive you with open arms.

To make this possible, Jesus has come and died in your place and has been raised from the dead. To receive salvation, you must acknowledge him and honor him as its source and basis. To do this, you must turn away from your sin in true repentance, and turn toward God and call upon the name of the Lord. This turning requires sincere faith in Jesus and a saving encounter with him in the waters of baptism.

All this together is the essential gospel. We cannot leave any of it out. Most of Christendom will agree with this, up to the very last point—about Christian baptism. But on this point, as all others, I would rather agree with Peter and Paul and Philip and God himself than the whole Christian world (Romans 3:4). It was good for Paul and Philip, and it's good enough for me.

---

[1] See my book, *Baptism: A Biblical Study* (College Press, 1989).

Fundamental #7

Jesus Is Coming Again

The term *eschatology* includes the doctrines about the end times, especially the second coming of Jesus. It includes events leading up to the second coming (such as the antichrist and tribulation) and following it (like the resurrection and judgment).

Few doctrines have divided Bible believers more than eschatology. Disagreements abound on practically every detail. Nevertheless there is one central belief on which they all agree: *Jesus is coming again*. This has always been one of the fundamentals or essentials.

The biblical view of history is unique in that it pictures history as linear, that is, as having a beginning and an end. In pagan thought, history is usually open-ended and ultimately cyclical. That is, on a cosmic and aeonic scale, history just keeps repeating itself. In contrast with this, the Bible says human history had a distinct beginning when God created the heavens and earth (Genesis 1:1). His goal was a race of freewill creatures who would voluntarily glorify him and gratefully enjoy his blessings forever.

Progress toward this goal was interrupted almost at once by the fall of Adam and Eve into sin. As a result, the earth and the whole human race came under the control of sin and death (Romans 5:12 ff.; 8:18 ff.). But this did not defeat God's purpose. He will achieve his goal by an alternate route—the way of salvation through Jesus Christ. Through his cross and resurrection, Jesus redeems and restores the creation, setting it on its current trajectory toward the original goal.

So cosmic history as we know it will end when God decides his goal has been reached. The climactic event that will accomplish this closure is the second coming of Jesus.

The Reality of Christ's Return

Regarding eschatology, the topic Bible believers argue most about is the kingdom of God, or the millennial kingdom. One controversial issue is its *nature:* is it a literal, physical kingdom, or is it a spiritual reign of Christ in men's hearts? Another issue is its *time* in relation to Christ's second coming. Will his coming precede the establishment of the kingdom on earth, and thus be premillennial? Or will his coming follow the kingdom, and thus be postmillennial?

These and similar questions have been the preoccupation of countless Christians, especially for the last century and a half. But even though the millennium is an *important* doctrine, it is not an *essential* one. I believe there is a correct view on this subject (the amillennial one, for the record), but this is not a view one has to accept in order to be a Christian. Redeemed people of every millennial stripe will be in heaven.

Fortunately, all Bible-believing millennial views agree on the core event around which all the other events must be arranged: the second coming of Jesus. They agree that one day the glorified, triumphant Messiah will break through the barrier separating the angelic heaven (Revelation 4, 5) from this physical cosmos, and that he will visibly enter this cosmos and bring all its current processes to an end and the human race to judgment. This is the seventh and final fundamental.

On the night before his death Jesus reassured his apostles with these words: "I will come again, and receive you to Myself; that where I am, there you may be also" (John 14:3). Forty days after his death and resurrection these same apostles watched Jesus ascend into heaven: "He was lifted up while they were looking on, and a cloud received Him out of their sight" (Acts 1:9). At this traumatic moment they received further reassurance from two angelic messengers:

And as they were gazing intently into the sky while He was departing, behold, two men in white clothing stood beside them; and they also said, "Men of Galilee, why do you stand looking into the sky? This Jesus, who has been taken up from you into heaven, will come in just the same way as you have watched Him go into heaven" (Acts 1:10, 11).

No doubt remembering these words and other words of Jesus, the apostle John declares, "Behold, He is coming with the clouds, and every eye will see Him, even those who pierced Him" (Revelation 1:7). John reminds us that "when He appears, we shall be like Him, because we shall see Him just as He is" (1 John 3:2). That is, we shall see him in his glorified body (Philippians 3:21), as the martyr Stephen saw him (Acts 7:56) and as Saul saw him on the Damascus road (Acts 9:3 ff.).

Because of such biblical testimony, Christians through the ages have believed that Jesus will return to earth in a literal, visible manner, and that everyone will actually see him in the same way we look into the sky *today* and see clouds overhead.

With the rise of liberalism in the late nineteenth century, however, this belief was called into question. Because it rejected the whole concept of the supernatural and any such interruption of the natural order, liberalism denied the whole idea of a visible return of Jesus that would bring history to an abrupt end. Liberal theologians limited Christian hope to a continuing spiritual presence of Jesus in the hearts of his followers. Jesus "comes again" every time someone accepts Jesus as his spiritual guide.

An example of someone who asserted this view is the popular liberal theologian, William Newton Clarke. He describes the second coming as "a perpetual advent, in which Christ comes ever more fully into the life of the world." It is a "spiritual and invisible coming by means of which his spiritual work in the world has been carried forward." Clarke states very clearly that "no visible return of Christ to the earth is to be expected, but rather the long and steady advance of his spiritual kingdom."[1]

In opposition to this heresy, the early fundamentalists included in their list of fundamentals not just the return of Jesus, but specifically his *visible, personal* coming. Nothing less can do justice to the biblical teaching.

Of course, there are still those who follow the liberal approach. They ridicule the idea of Christ's visible return. Richard Bowman reports listening to a taped lecture by a seminary professor who said, "To preach that Jesus will literally return to earth is unintelligible to modern man. Therefore, we must not preach it." It is impossible, he said, for Jesus to return in such a way that every eye could see him simultaneously from all sides of the globe. Some people might even hurt their necks trying to get a good look![2]

Such a denial goes much deeper than just problems with logistics. The real issue is whether or not we believe the supernatural is real, the Bible is true, and Jesus is Lord. If we believe these things, we won't have any problem believing in Christ's visible return. (By the way, the Bible does not say that every eye shall see him *simultaneously*. Once earthly activity has come to a standstill, Christ could make several majestic orbits around the globe while his angel choir fills the whole sky and heralds his presence.)

The Details of Christ's Return

Christ's second coming will be accompanied by several other crucial events that both precede and follow it. In this section I will summarize this series of events as I understand them.

Before His Coming

The time just preceding the second coming will be a time of intense spiritual warfare. It is a time when an "antichrist" will prevail in an unprecedented way. There are many antichrists, and they have been present ever since the first century (1 John 2:18-22; 4:3; 2 John 7). But the second coming will be preceded by an especially powerful one, also called the "man of lawlessness" (2 Thessalonians 2:3-12). His "coming is in accord with the activity of Satan, with all power and signs and false wonders" (2 Thessalonians 2:9). This is the time of the loosing of Satan (Revelation 20:3, 7-9).

Satan was bound at the first coming of Jesus through the preaching of the gospel (Matthew 12:22-30; Revelation 20:1-6). During the church age God restrains the forces of sin and lawlessness, but a time will come when he withdraws his restraint (2 Thessalonians 2:7). This will be shortly before the end of time and the second coming (2 Thessalonians 2:3, 8; Revelation 20:9).

Exactly how long Satan will be loose is uncertain. Revelation 20:3 calls it a "short time," in comparison with the length of the church age.

What will this time be like? It will be an intense spiritual battle (Ephesians 6:12). Satan's forces will attack us primarily with *falsehood*, in a battle for our minds. The devil will "come out to deceive the nations" (Revelation 20:8) through "deceitful spirits and doctrines of demons" (1 Timothy 4:1). He will hurl "all the deception of wickedness" at those who "did not receive the love of the truth so as to be saved" (2 Thessalonians 2:10).

It will also be a time of great *wickedness*, a battle for our wills. Falsehood leads to apostasy, lawlessness, and indulging in wickedness (2 Thessalonians 2:3-12). The doctrines of demons lead to hardened consciences and extremely wicked sins and lifestyles (1 Timothy 4:1-5; 2 Timothy 3:1-5).

It may also be a time of *persecution*, perhaps a battle for our very lives. Most people associate this time with tribulation of one kind or another. Revelation 20:9 makes it clear that God's people will be the object of attack. Whether this is limited to spiritual warfare or also includes physical persecution is not clear. At the very least Christians can expect to be under great pressure socially and culturally.

Are we presently in this time of the loosing of Satan? Maybe, maybe not. This answer is not a cop-out. I believe the biblical descriptions of the events preceding the "end times" are deliberately ambiguous on God's part. They are general enough that Christians of all ages may consider themselves to be close to the end. The age in which we live certainly qualifies. This enables us to say, not, "The end *is* near," but "The end *may be* near."

His Coming

We have already described the visible nature of Christ's return. Other details may be learned by examining the three main New Testament words describing this event. First, his coming will be an *appearing* (Greek, *epiphaneia*). Titus 2:13 speaks of "the appearing of the glory of our great God and Savior." In ancient Greece this term was used for the official arrival of rulers. In this case it is the arrival or appearing of the King of Kings.

One thing emphasized by the use of this term is suddenness or unexpectedness. Christ's appearing is compared with a thief in the night (1 Thessalonians 5:2). Jesus said it will be at "an hour when you do not think" (Matthew 24:44). Many will be preoccupied with worldly things and will be taken by surprise. Thus Jesus commands us to *watch*—to be alert and ready. "Therefore be on the alert, for you do not know which day your Lord is coming" (Matthew 24:42).

Even for those watching, it will still be sudden. It will be like watching for lightning in the sky during a storm. Though you are watching, still it is so sudden that you are surprised. It is expected, yet unexpected. Thus it shall be with Christ. All at once, he will *appear*.

Second, Christ's coming will be a *revelation* (Greek, *apokalypsis*). We are "awaiting eagerly the revelation of our Lord Jesus Christ" (1 Corinthians 1:7), the "revelation of His glory" (1 Peter 4:13). It will be like an unveiling. In the imagery of Revelation 6:14, "the sky was split apart like a scroll when it is rolled up," like curtains being drawn open.

This is in contrast with the outward humiliation that characterized his first coming, and the present hiddenness of his glory from the eyes of the world. In that final day his glory and majesty will be revealed to all. He will be revealed as King of Kings and Lord of Lords (Revelation 19:16). As 2 Thessalonians 1:7 says, "The Lord Jesus shall be revealed from heaven with His mighty angels in flaming fire."

Third, Christ's return will be his *coming* or *presence* (Greek, *parousia*). In 1 Thessalonians 3:13 Paul prays that God may establish our hearts as "unblamable . . . at the coming of our Lord Jesus with all His saints." This word indicates a coming that is not just a quick visit, but one that results in the Savior's abiding presence with us. He will return to be present in our midst, personally and visibly.

There is no doubt that the second coming will be the greatest spectacle the universe has ever known. In addition to the great visual display that every eye will see, there will be sounds heard by every ear. "For the Lord Himself will descend from heaven with a shout, with the voice of the archangel, and with the trumpet of God" (1 Thessalonians 4:16).

The content of the Lord's shout is not given. ("Time's up"? "Ready or not, here I come"?) The voice of the archangel may be the words of Revelation 11:15, "The kingdom of the world has become the kingdom of our Lord, and of His Christ; and He will reign forever and ever." "The last trumpet" is also mentioned in 1 Corinthians 15:52. (See Matthew 24:31.)

The particular response we make will depend on our relationship to the Lord at the time of his coming. The wicked will try to flee and hide (Revelation 6:15-17), but Christ will destroy them: "Fire came down from heaven and devoured them" (Revelation 20:9; see 2 Thessalonians 1:7-9; 2:8). God's people, however, will rejoice (1 Peter 4:13). Ultimately, whether grudgingly or gladly, every knee will bow and every tongue will confess that Jesus Christ is Lord (Philippians 2:9-11).

After His Coming

A series of glorious events will begin as soon as Jesus makes his appearance. The first two occur very close together, namely, the resurrection and the raptures.

Some Bible believers are confused on these two events. They expect one rapture and two bodily resurrections. Most if not all premillennialists believe that at Christ's return there will be *one* rapture—of Christians only, plus the first of two bodily resurrections—this one of Christians only. Then, following the millennium, comes the second bodily resurrection—of the wicked only.

Scripture gives us a different picture, however. In the end times there are *one* resurrection and *two* raptures.

Actually there *are* two resurrections, but the first is not an end-time event. It is a spiritual resurrection that occurs at baptism (John 5:25; Romans 6:3-5; Colossians 2:12). Only those who become Christians experience this first resurrection. The second resurrection is of the body, and it happens to both the righteous and the wicked at the return of Jesus. At that time all the dead will be raised together, each having the body that will be his or hers for eternity (John 5:28, 29; Acts 24:15).

Some misunderstand the statement in 1 Thessalonian 4:16, "The dead in Christ shall rise first." They assume this is in contrast with the sinners, who will rise at a later time. But this is not the point of comparison. The *dead* in Christ rise first, then the *living* in Christ will be changed into their new bodies without experiencing either death or resurrection as such. The point is the same as 1 Corinthians 15:51, 52: "We shall not all sleep, but we shall all be changed, in a moment, in the twinkling of an eye, at the last trumpet; for the trumpet will sound, and the dead will be raised imperishable, and we shall be changed."

The resulting scene is this: Earth's surface is crowded with people in their raised and changed bodies, believers and unbelievers mingled together—but not for long. The stage is set for the next event: the raptures.

The word *rapture* in this context literally describes the physical action of "catching up, snatching away." It contains no connotation of sublime feelings. It is totally different from the way the word is used in poetic contexts, like "when with rapture I behold him." It comes from the Latin word used to translate "caught up" in 1 Thessalonians 4:17.

Yes, there *will* be a rapture! But here is a little-observed and usually ignored biblical teaching: there will be *two* raptures. One is a snatching away of the wicked; the other is a snatching away of believers. And the most shocking fact of all is that the wicked are raptured first.

The parable of the tares in Matthew 13:24-30 makes this clear. Here, Jesus specifically says the tares (sinners) are gathered first by his angels at the end of the world: "First gather up the tares" (v. 30). We know this is what it means because Jesus himself interprets the parable for us in verses 37-43. "Therefore just as the tares are gathered up and burned with fire, so shall it be at the end of the age" (v. 40). Revelation 14:14-20 confirms this.

But what about the passage that says, "One will be taken, and one will be left" (Matthew 24:37-41)? The problem is that we have just assumed that the saved are taken and the wicked are left. But Jesus said, "The coming of the Son of Man will be just like the days of Noah" (v. 37), when the flood came and took the *wicked* away (v. 39). Following this analogy, we must conclude that at the end the one taken first is the sinner and the one left is the saint.

So here is the sequence: After the resurrection and change have been completed, the wicked are then caught up and removed from the earth, leaving the righteous standing alone. Only at that point does their rapture occur, as all are "caught up together . . . in the clouds to meet the Lord in the air" (1 Thessalonians 4:17). This is the rapture many Christians are eagerly looking for. Many have simply misunderstood when and how and why it takes place.

This raises a good question. Both the wicked and the righteous have now been raptured, taken up from a now-empty earth. But raptured to where? And why? Where do we go after leaving the earth? And why is the earth left empty? These questions are answered in two subsequent events that occur simultaneously.

The first of these two events is the renewal of the universe by fire. The main reason God evacuates the dimension of physical space is so he can set the whole thing on fire (2 Peter 3:10-12). This fiery holocaust does not necessarily annihilate the universe. It may simply renew and purify it, or purge it of its sin-caused impurities. In any case, the result is a *new* heavens (outer space) and a *new* earth, which will be the eternal home of the righteous. See Isaiah 65:17; 66:22; 2 Peter 3:13; Revelation 21:1.

So the purpose of rapturing everyone from the earth is not to rescue believers from some great tribulation, but to empty the physical universe of *all* human beings so this purification and renewal can take place.

The second of these two simultaneous events is the final judgment. When human beings are raptured out of this universe, they are transported through the dimensional barrier into the very throne room of God. So while the earthly dimension is undergoing its fiery renovation, the human race is gathered before the judgment throne in the angelic dimension.

There is only one final judgment (Revelation 11:18). It involves all people, good and bad (sheep and goats), at the same time. The goats are arranged to the left of the throne, the sheep to the right (Matthew 25:31-33). In Revelation 20:12, 13, "the dead" refers to all of the dead.

This judgment has several purposes.

It is a public *separation* of the good and the bad, whereas in this life all remain together (Matthew 13:24-30).

It is a public *examination* of the records of all, so that God may be shown to be completely fair and just, and no respecter of persons. Thus all are judged according to their deeds (2 Corinthians 5:10; Revelation 22:12).

It is also a public *vindication* of God's justice and mercy.

Finally it is a public *allocation* of rewards and punishments. See Matthew 11:22, 24; Mark 12:40; Luke 12:47, 48; 19:11-27; 20:47; 2 Corinthians 9:6.

The final eschatological event is the inauguration of the eternal states. The wicked are condemned to eternal torment in hell (Revelation 20:14, 15), but God has something wonderful in store for believers.

I picture a scene like this: Judgment is over and the wicked have been removed. We remain gazing in awe at our Savior and eternal companion, Jesus. Then he says, "Turn around and look!" We turn and see this huge city of golden glory (Revelation 21:10-21). Jesus says, "I've been preparing this for you. Go inside." And all the saved enter this great city.

But that's not the end. Jesus says, "Hang on! We're going for a ride." And this great city, the New Jerusalem, starts on a journey. To what destination? Through the dimensional barrier, back to the new earth. The apostle John describes this event from the perspective of the new earth in Revelation 21:1, 2:

> And I saw a new heaven and a new earth; for the first heaven and the first earth passed away, and there is no longer any sea [on the new earth]. And I saw the holy city, new Jerusalem, coming down out of heaven from God, made ready as a bride adorned for her husband.

As it slowly descends to its resting place on the new earth, I can imagine countless heads peeking out the windows, uttering lots of oohs and ahs at the beautiful new universe.

Then the holy city comes to rest upon the new earth, which will be our eternal home. What? Not in *heaven?* Well, actually, it *is* heaven, since heaven by definition is wherever God is. Revelation 21:3 says that God makes the new earth his own home: "Now the dwelling of God is with men, and he will live with them" *(New International Version).* So in a sense we do not "go to heaven"; heaven comes to us!

No wonder Paul said, "Therefore, my beloved brethren, be steadfast, immovable, always abounding in the work of the Lord, knowing that your toil is not in vain in the Lord" (1 Corinthians 15:58).

The Essentiality of Christ's Return

Why is the doctrine of Christ's second coming a bull's-eye belief? Why is it an essential part of the Christian faith? Why can't a person deny the second coming and still be a Christian? Is anything crucial really at stake here?

There are at least three reasons why this is an essential doctrine. First, Christ's return is necessary in order to vindicate God, his purpose and his plan. Ever since the beginning (Genesis 3:15), God has been promising redemption and eternal life for believers and vengeance upon his enemies. Will it ever happen? Is it all a delusion and a false hope? Are we as Christians wasting our time and energy "living for Jesus"?

While Noah was building the ark and preaching repentance in view of the coming flood, the people ignored him (Matthew 24:38), and no doubt they mocked him too. But he kept at his task for 120 years (Genesis 6:3 ff.), and God finally vindicated himself and Noah's own steadfast faith by sending the promised flood.

In a like manner people mock the promise and expectation of Christ's second coming, saying, "Where is the promise of His coming? For ever since the fathers fell asleep, all continues just as it was from the beginning of creation" (2 Peter 3:4). But "the day of the Lord will come," says Peter (v. 10). God has promised, and we believe his promise.

In the movie *E.T.*, when Elliott tried to tell his older brother that he had an alien in his closet, he was ridiculed with a "sure you do!" attitude. In the TV sitcom *Different Strokes*, Arnold discovered and tried to report drug trafficking in his school; but no one would believe him—until Nancy Reagan appeared on the scene.

At times Christians may feel like Elliott and Arnold. We proclaim our faith: "Jesus is Lord. He is God. He rose from the dead. He saved me from my sins. He is coming again." And we hear all around us, in so many words, "Sure, sure. You Christians! You're so stupid, so ignorant!"

Sometimes we ourselves may be tempted to doubt. After all, the world is so pagan, and we have been waiting nearly two thousand years. We cry out with the martyrs, "How long, O Lord?" (Revelation 6:10).

Unless Jesus comes again, the mockers will win. If he does not return, our faith is in vain. The alleged plan of redemption, thousands of years in the works, will turn out to be phony. The anti-supernaturalists will be vindicated. All the so-called "essentials" will be myths after all.

But the return of Jesus will be one big "I told you so!" both for God and for Christians. God will thus vindicate himself one final time: "Let God be found true, though every man be found a liar, as it is written, 'That Thou mightest be justified in Thy words, and mightest prevail when Thou art judged'" (Romans 3:4). Christians' faith will also be vindicated with the revelation of Jesus' lordship. When everyone sees Jesus riding across the sky with the angelic armies following, his robe emblazoned with "King of Kings, and Lord of Lords" (Revelation 19:11-16), it will be hard not to shout, "See? You see? It's true! I told you so!"

Second, Christ's return is necessary in order to uphold the integrity of God's physical creation. In nonbiblical world views, the physical universe is either an accident or a mistake. But according to the Bible, it is the deliberate creation of God and thus is part of his purpose for mankind. The tragedy is that sin has perverted and corrupted not just human life but the whole universe (Romans 8:18-23).

Those who believe the world originated through purely natural processes (such as a mysterious "big bang") believe it will continue to operate according to those processes until it eventually runs down and enters a state of universal, permanent inertia. The world will then be one big cosmic junk pile. Many Christians have been influenced by this and other pagan world views, and have come to think of the universe as just a temporary stage in human development, something that will be discarded when we advance on to "heaven."

Such is not the case, however. Christ will return to redeem not just his people but his entire creation. As Peter proclaimed in Acts 3:21, Jesus' return will be "the period of restoration of all things." Out of the cosmic holocaust will emerge "new heavens and a new earth, in which righteousness dwells" (2 Peter 3:13). All the effects of sin will be burned away, and the renewed creation will be ready to serve God's eternal purpose.

Third, Christ's return is necessary to guarantee the accountability of man. God created us with free will, but how can we be held accountable for our choices? The answer is the final judgment. When Jesus comes again, one of his main purposes will be to bring every responsible person into judgment.

Is this really an essential part of the Christian message? In his sermon to Cornelius, the apostle Peter described God's commission to preach Christ: "He ordered us to preach to the people, and solemnly to testify that this is the One who has been appointed by God as Judge of the living and the dead" (Acts 10:42). When he preached to the Athenians, Paul declared that God "has fixed a day in which He will judge the world in righteousness through a Man whom He has appointed, having furnished proof to all men by raising Him from the dead" (Acts 17:31).

Hebrews 11:6 declares that acceptable, pleasing faith must include not just a belief that God exists, but also "that He is a rewarder of those who seek Him." The emphasis in this verse is on God's reward to the faithful. This is a reward according to grace (Romans 4:4), in reality a gift (Romans 6:23). But the coming

Judge will also bring the reward earned by unrepentant sinners, the eternal "wages of doing wrong" (2 Peter 2:13; see Romans 6:23). Thus Jesus declares, "Behold, I am coming quickly, and My reward is with Me, to render to every man according to what he has done" (Revelation 22:12).

Yes, Jesus is coming again. And yes, this is an essential aspect of Christian belief. It is a fitting capstone and climactic doctrine rounding out the list of faith's fundamentals:

1. Truth Itself Is Fundamental
2. God Is Real
3. The Bible Is God's Word
4. Jesus Is Our Savior
5. Jesus Is God's Son
6. We Are Saved by Grace, Through Faith, in Baptism
7. Jesus Is Coming Again

[1] William Newton Clarke, *An Outline of Christian Theology* (Edinburgh: T. and T. Clark, 1899), 443–444.

[2] Richard M. Bowman, "The Exalted Christ," *Disciple Renewal* (July/August 1994), 12.